Healthy Mind, Body, & Soul

Finding Hope in a Hurting Marriage

Daphney Wright

Copyright © 2020 Daphney Wright

All rights reserved. No part of this book may be reproduced in any form or by any electronic or mechanical means, including information storage and retrieval systems, without permission in writing from the publisher, except by reviewers, who may quote brief passages in a review.

ISBN: 978-1-7323811-9-3

Printed in the United States of America

Story Corner Publishing LLC.

6024 Churchland Blvd. suite 10

Portsmouth, VA 23703

Storycornerpublishing@yahoo.com

Dedication

I want the world to know that I could not have completed this book, especially in a timely matter without a few good people who I hold dear to my heart. Walter Wright if it had not been for God on our sides, I do not know where we would be. I love you for giving up your time so that I could go back to school to finish my degree. Thank you for your love and support. To my daughters who had to give up their mother sometimes, I know it was not easy, thank you. Also, to my family when they heard me say, "I got schoolwork to do," thank you for your patience and understanding when I didn't show up to the cookout and countless other events.To my friends and family, who told me, "I can't wait to read your book," thank you for believing in me and having my back.

Contents

Preface 1
Acknowledgement 2
Introduction 3
7 Tips for Godly Wives, Mothers, & Myself 5
Finding Hope in My Marriage 10
What's Your Emotional Love Language? 12
Communication in Marriage 13
Marriage Gods' Way 16
The Gift of Servitude 19
Take Your Power Back 21
Obligated or Commanded 23
Sacrifice or Obedience 25
Falling in Love versus Walking in Love 27
Anger Management 29
Temptations in the Marriage 31
Forgiveness 33
Provider 35
Put Jesus Back on the Throne 37
Sustainability 39
Spiritual Maturity 41
Rejection Builds Character 43
Pain Is A Teacher 45
Fear 47
Offended 49
Familiarity I 51
Familiarity II 53
Let it Go 57
Love Covers a Multitude of Sins 59
No Lack 61
Stress 62
Dignity 64

Unequally Yoked	66
Worship	68
Betrayal and Rejection	70
Insecurities	72
Adaptability	74
A Prisoner in Your Own Home	77
When they want your Stuff, but they do not Want You	79
Marriage or Roommate	81
Living versus Existing	83
Co-dependency	85
Believe	89
Victim Mindset versus Kingdom Mindset	91
Mistreated	93
Prophesy	94
Life is not a Sprint or a Marathon	96
Title versus Entitled	98
Escalates versus De-Escalates	100
Be Still	102
Let us Get Back to the Basics	104
Depression	106
Choosing My Own Way	108

Preface

My name is Daphney Wright. I have been married to my husband Walter for fifteen years. We are both born and raised in Philadelphia, Pennsylvania.

We have two daughters, and five grandchildren who are all under the age of nine. Over the past fifteen years, I realized that I constantly rely on my faith in God, to help me to take care of my family, and most importantly to take care of me.

As a Godly wife, I most certainly can relate to feeling burdened. Being in the state of stress for a very long time, can put a strain on your body, and as a result the body starts to break down. Godly women must learn how to take care of themselves first and then others.

My goal is to inspire not only Godly wives. I want to teach wives how to grow in their spiritual life and stand strong on the promises of God in the face of adversity. Spiritual growth sounds challenging, but is needed for us to grow into marriage.

Providing tips for Godly wives on how to take their focus off their problems and put it on God who will ultimately heal every broken place in their lives. Until we learn how to take care of ourselves, will be no good for our family. To help wives to endure and persevere in their marriages, I will teach them how to apply God's Word to their lives.

I will be sharing a bit of my own testimony by talking about the battles of life that fight me as a Godly wife, how I endured, and persevere through them.

Acknowledgement

First and foremost, I must acknowledge "The All Mighty God." Thank you for allowing me the opportunity to share with other like-minded women who need to know the power of God on the inside of them. I have learned so much through my marriage. I want you to know that marriage is not a bad thing, but it is a God thing. Couples just need the necessary tools, to keep the marriage working in God's order. We must get our perspectives right and get our priorities in order, Godly wives.

Last, but not least, I thank my family, friends, and church family for being such a great influence in my life. You do not know how much you have been a part of this journey with me. I am so grateful to God for all of you and how you have touched my heart so deeply and have been a great deal of support to me.

Introduction

This book is to encourage the Godly woman in her marriage. There are a lot of hurting marriages out in the world. We as woman often focus entirely on what the world's view of marriage is and not what God intended marriage to be.

As a woman, God wants to know how are you, where are you, and how can He help? Godly women focus so much on the marriage that they lose themselves. Women need to return to their first love- God. Jesus Christ died on an old rugged cross to give us life abundantly.

Often, we forget that He created us to be woman first and foremost, then He created us for purpose on purpose. Women need to be nurtured, cultivated, loved, protected, and provided for. These are all the things a good father does for his daughter. She is the apple of his eye. There is no good thing that he will withhold from his children.

God loves us so much, He does not want to see us hurt, mistreated, or broken. He wants the very best for His daughters. What parent would not want the best for their children? Let God love on you to get you back to who He created you to be and with a purpose, His perfect will for your life.

This book will focus on the following:

1. You were created as a woman
2. The woman was created for purpose
3. Knowing who you are in Christ
4. Walking in your God given authority

5. Finding hope in a hurting marriage
6. Be transformed in your mind
7. Preparing your hands for war

These are just a few to get you started on your journey and to ignite the power within you. Godly wife, you were created for purpose. As a woman, you are Satan's direct target. You were created to bruise the head of the serpent, in other words, to annihilate the works of the enemy. God needs you to spiritually mature so that He can use you for His good. Satan desires to use you for his evil.

The bible states choose whom this day you will serve. Knowing who you are and why you were created will help you to know your purpose while here on earth. God wants to partner with you to get you to your destiny.

What has God spoken to you or over your life? I remember the day when God told me that I was pregnant with ministry, a book, a business. He wants you to manifest His desires for you in the earth, these are the good works He created you to do before the foundations of the earth. He knew you when you were in your mother's womb. Your legacy is at risk if you do not receive God's will for your life. I hope you are encouraged Godly wife.

7 Tips for Godly Wives, Mothers, & Myself

Ladies, I have learned that being a Godly wife is not always easy. We wear many hats—woman, wife, mother, grandmother, godmother, aunt, sister, and friend. I have compiled a list of resources below that I currently use in my daily walk with God. These tips have blessed me immensely:

Communicate

Men and women communicate differently. Men think in compartments which means, they can only process one thing at a time, but women think about a few things all at once because we are multi-taskers. A good friend explained to me that men's brains are like waffles—you pour the syrup in one square at a time. Simply let your husband process the first question before you give him the second question. Men want to be respected above all things in a marriage. Women want conversation to help her feel safe and secure.

"According to the Wiki summaries on *Men from Mars, Women from Venus by John Gray,* in Chapter 5: Speaking Different Languages, Men talk in very literal terms for the purpose of relaying information; women employ artistic license and a dramatic vocabulary to fully express and relate their feelings." Often in relationships communication is one of our biggest problems. I believe, this is an area where will always be a work in progress.

Take Care of You

We need to treat ourselves at least once a week by going out to the movies, nail salon, hair salon, breakfast, lunch, dinner, and do not forget to get a massage every now and then. Please visit Groupon Website to sign-up for free and you will receive awesome discounts that will come in handy. If you just cannot simply get away, run yourself a hot bath with plenty of bubbles once everything is calm at home. Know that God wants us to put Him first in our lives not our spouses. Secondly, God wants us to learn how to love ourselves before we can love anyone else.

Alleviating Stress

Alleviating stress is to get to the root of the problem, whether it is your husband complaining about the finances, the kids did not clean their room, or you are too busy to spend any time with your husband. Someone, please feed the dog! Wives, please get to the root of the problem by deciding when it is a good time to sit down and talk to your husband, instead of allowing things to build up inside of you.

Read Your Bible

How is your spiritual life? Are you a believer? Do you have a relationship with God? Well, if you do not, there is no time like now to start seeking God. One way you can do this is by reading His word. The Bible has a scripture that He will meet you right where you are in life, but first ask God to speak to your heart.

There are stories in the Bible that you and your spouse can relate to. You can download the Bible App on your personal computer, iPad, Tablet, iPhone, or Android phone. The Bible App has numerous devotions/plans that will help you to grow spiritually, thus creating an intimate relationship with God. These devotions/plans teach you how to apply God's word to your life by believing and trusting in God that He will do what His word says He will do. God's promises in the bible are "Yes" and "Amen!"

Quiet Time

Learn how to take time each day to sit alone with God through prayer and meditation. Know when you seek God for a specific purpose, you will find Him. It is hard to quiet our minds after a busy day of work, but you can ask God for help in this area. Try to incorporate fasting and praying into your life, especially, when you seek God for something. We all need God's help and guidance in life. You may need help with your husband, the children, yourself, or someone else. God is right there with you. Listen for God's answer and walk by faith, not by sight.

Seek Daily Inspiration

There are so many well-known pastors who inspire and encourage me along my journey as a wife. You can sign-up for daily inspirations from various ministries in the world via email. Sharing with other wives really helps to spread the good news. Most of these pastors have their own social media pages. You can even see a full sermon on YouTube, I Need a Word Network, Trinity Broadcast Network, and of course Facebook.

Be Patient

Learning your spouse can be challenging at times, but if you both commit to the process the relationship will grow. It takes time to come up with conflict resolutions for your marriage. Be patient because it will not happen overnight. The Bible gives us great scriptures on whatever we are dealing with in our marriages or our everyday lives.

I know firsthand that we often, as wives, do not have time to read. My favorite scripture that I learned was, "Your word is a lamp unto my feet and a light unto my path." Learning how to apply God's word to our daily lives can be simple. We must transform our minds by the washing of the word of God. We all can find serenity in knowing who we are in Christ.

I decided to give these seven tips because spiritually it represents completion. I hope that you find the same help and inspiration from these tips as I do. Praying for healthy minds, bodies, and souls of all God's people. I leave you with this scripture, "The Joy of the Lord is My Strength."

Communication is Key

The first year of our marriage communication became less and by the second year even lesser. I know you are wondering what happened and we will explore that later. The point I want to get across here is, if the marriage has great communication, there is nothing that you and your spouse cannot accomplish together.

Compassion

You must have a deep compassion for meeting your spouse's needs. God wants us to meet our spouse's needs. Helping our spouse to grow is our jobs as wives; we are the helpmate. There is a time and a place to communicate a message to your spouse. Ladies, often we have been home caring for the children, cooking, cleaning, and have had time to write a "To Do List" for the house. Wives is not good, if your husband worked all day, the last thing he wants to do is go over a "To Do List."

Give him time. Let him eat dinner, spend some time with the children, watch the basketball game, and maybe half time will be a more suitable time to talk about the "To Do List." Finding the appropriate time to talk to your spouse is important. A woman who learns her house, learns her spouse.

Communication becomes less and less when you only focus on all the negative things about your spouse. Walter and I were good friends. We thought we would not encounter any problems with communication in our marriage. After all, we knew everything there was to know about each other. Well, this was the problem. Like a horse, once the blinders were off, we wanted to take off running. We learned not to communicate as much as we use to as a form of protection. Wives, God has all the protection we will ever need.

The Onion Analogy

For Walter and me, silence became golden as a form of protection. We thought this would cut down on the amount of arguments, but we were so wrong. To get my husband to talk was like peeling a strong onion, one layer at a time. I would ask my husband things like, "What's wrong? What did I do? Why are you acting like that? If you can imagine, he was always on the defense.

My tone of voice was that of a parole officer, not a compassionate and loving wife. I had to learn how to speak to my husband and it was not easy. God was dealing with my heart. The way I was raised was to ask a question if I do not know something. Walter hated being questioned. We had to come to an understanding and the only way we could do that was to communicate instead of reading each other's minds. Communication is and always will be key.
Ladies with the right scriptures being applied to your heart, you too can change the way you communicate with your spouse. Here are a few scriptures that will help:

A Kind Word (Proverbs 16:24)

A Noble Wife (Proverb 31:10)

Wives/Husbands (1 Peter 3)

Finding Hope in My Marriage

Negative emotions can way heavy on a person's heart. Learning how to be led by the Holy Spirit and not by the flesh is something we must ask God to help us with. Did you know that negative emotions hinder your blessings and your walk with God?

Walking around with hidden anger only builds up until you explode. Due to a motor vehicle accident my husband was out of work for a while. If you can imagine, the worries of life came tumbling down on me hard and I exploded.

My husband and I got into a heated argument. I went upstairs to sit quietly to think about what I had done. I began to read a devotional which told me to put off all malice, rage, bitterness, and anger because these things do not please God. These things did not produce the righteousness of God.

We all need to look at the bigger picture when it comes to our emotions because they will lead us down the road of despair, hurt, disappointments, unmet expectations, and pain. God wants to lead us to peace, unspeakable joy, and happiness.

God began to show me that the bills were paid, food was on the table, and gas was in the car. He showed me how He has been providing for us all alone. I could not do anything but ask for God's forgiveness and apologize to my husband. There is a scripture that I meditated on, Psalms 23:1, "The Lord is my Shepherd, I Shall Not Want."

God is our hope! The Bible tells us a story about a Samaritan woman at the well, John 4:1-42; this story gives hope to women that are lost. There is nothing too great or beyond repair that God cannot fix.

God has a purpose for each one of us. When we go through trials and tribulations, they help to teach us something about ourselves, others, and God. Trials helps us to correct an unknown sin and shape our character. When we work on ourselves this takes the focus off our circumstances and puts it on God.

What's Your Emotional Love Language?

"Five Ways to Love Your Spouse"

"The Five Love Languages" by Gary Chapman, PhD, is a really good book that helped me and my husband. We read this book a few years back and it really helped get us through some tough communication barriers. Chapman talks about the five emotional love languages we are to exemplify in our marriages. Once couples become aware of their nature of love, they can speak a language that their spouse can understand to meet their needs.

After reading the book, we each took out a pen and a piece of paper. We wrote down the five love languages in the order we personally thought it should be and switched papers. This was a very good and interesting exercise that all married couples should do. I recommend this resource. The Five love Languages are as follows: Acts of Service, Quality Time, Physical Touch, Words of Affirmation, and Receiving Gifts.

Marriage is beautiful and it works, but each spouse must be willing to do their part. Learning how to communicate with your spouse emotionally and physically increases your intimacy in your marriage. Know that the enemy of our Godly marriages wants nothing more than to divide us and steal our intimacy. Please hold on, God is the center of your marriage, and He is that third cord that is not easily broken. Here are a few scriptures to help you on your marriage journey:

Proverb 18.21

Ephesians 6:12

Proverbs 31:10-31

Ephesians 5:25-33

Communication in Marriage

Mirror Effect

To mutually understand one another in a marriage is important. A couple of years ago, my husband and I took a "Mastering the Mystery of Love" class that taught us a key component of communication which is the 'mirror effect'. He would communicate something to me, and I would repeat it back to him. For example, my husband will say, "I tell you over and over what I need, and you do not take heed to it." I would say, "Correct me if I am wrong, you said, "I am not a good listener, therefore, what you say to me goes in one ear and out the other."

We often do not take the time to listen to what our husbands are complaining about with the busyness of our day. Wives, this is an easy fix, just use the 'mirror effect' and nine times out of ten, it works. Mirroring helps you not only to connect with your husband, but to communicate and understand him to meet his needs.

Team Effort

Effective communication starts with a sender, message, and a receiver or listener. It does not matter which spouse is the sender or listener in the relationship if it is a team effort. Wives remember there is no 'I' in 'Team'. Both spouses must learn how to be a team player and have each other's back in everything that they do. Our husbands need to know that we are behind them one hundred percent. Wives, we just want to feel a sense of connectedness as we want to know what is going on and how we can help. When we do not communicate with our spouses, we tend to get caught up in our emotions and explode.

Listening

I have learned to be a good listener, believe it or not. Men just want to be heard and respected. When my husband is talking, I have learned to sit down, and give him my undivided attention. Being an active listener means both spouses need to put down their cell phones, turn the television off, and listen by hearing each other out one at a time. I have learned to listen by having direct eye-contact with my husband. Here are two very good scriptures that have helped me:

Proverbs 18:13

James 1:19

Be Empathetic

Try to see things from your husband's point of view before you start to judge him. Do not assume you know your husband's mindset and how a situation will pan-out. The worst thing we can say as a wife is, "I told you so." Remember this acronym, "ASSUME," assuming makes an "Ass out of U and Me," this is so true. We do not want to assume anything about our husbands, but to give them the benefit of the doubt. Wives please extend to your husbands the same grace that God extends to you.

Forgiveness

Forgiving your spouse for hurting you can be difficult. You forgive by telling your spouse, "I forgive you," but the very thing that hurt you still chips away at your heart. Please cast your cares upon God for He cares for you. If something is eating away at you like a cancer on the inside, confession is good for the soul. By confessing your sins to God and one another, you are saying, "God, I cannot handle it, please help me to forgive from the heart." You are setting your spouse free and receiving healing from God for yourself. Wives, leave the past in the past, do not bring up old things after you have forgiven your spouse, that is the trick of the enemy.

Give Him Time

If your husband is not communicating with you for a couple of days, just give him time to come around. Sometimes he needs his space. Your husband will handle problems differently than you will. For instance, you may get over something instantly, but it will take your husband a couple of days to let things go.

Be patient wives, your husbands will initiate conversation when he feels safe enough to share. Do not try to manipulate him into talking because you will just make a bigger mess. Just know that when it is the right time, you will know, but it will come in God's timing. I often pray during a time of miscommunication (silence) for unity and intimacy, when I feel distant from my husband. Are you a good listener or are you a good talker? Here is a great scripture that will help, Ephesians 4:3.

Marriage Gods' Way

Trust

Wives, learning to trust God is the key to every area of your life. God is the only one who can change the heart of man. You cannot or are you responsible for changing your spouse. Going to God and trusting Him to change you is the first key. Wives please, know that your circumstances may not change, but you will change in them. God sees your circumstances, but He is interested in you. He wants to have a loving relationship with you.

Relationship

Relationships matter to God a great deal and that is a fact of life. God is a relational God and He is the author of marriage. Marriage is a special anointing and not everyone can handle this gift. Know that you were anointed and stamped approved by God for your marriage. No one else can wear your shoes like you can. God chose you before the foundations of the earth.

Wives know that relationships are important, but they should not distract or hinder you in your walk with God. He is a jealous God who is madly in love with you. God wants us to be transformed into the likeness of His son, Jesus Christ. We are to look like God, love like God, respond like God, and react like God. Being mature in our emotions, says a lot about our character (who we are). We should not be tossed to and from because we do not have self-control. Know that our relationships glorify God.

Focus

Learning how to see your husband as Christ simply means take your focus off him and put it on God. He will lead you into sweet victory every time. I remember always complaining about my husband. Constant thoughts ran through my mind about what he did and what he did not do. One day, I heard God say in His still yet small voice, "What about you and what role did you play in all this?" Wives, you know that it takes two to tangle. Our husbands are not our enemies, neither are we their enemies.

Covenant

Remember your covenant between you, God, and your husband. On your special day, you and your husband were standing at the altar. You both looked into each other eyes and made a vow in the presence of God, family, and friends. You must always remember what you promised God.

Order

God is a God of order. Wives, your house must be in order:

- First, both spouses need to serve God with all their heart, mind, and soul (Authority).
- Secondly, the husband is charged with being the head of the house and the spiritual leader.
- Thirdly, the wife is charged with being the help meet, center of the home, and to encourage and build up her husband.
- Next, family is husband and wife training up the children in the way that they shall go and never depart from it.
- Lastly, God gives the husband and wife power to obtain wealth through creativity.

If your house is not in order, Satan comes to steal, kill, and destroy. In other words, a house divided cannot stand. Husbands need to band together wives to take care of family and home. Wives, we know all too well that a wise wife builds her home and a foolish wife tears her home down.

Encourage

Wives, encouragement was the very thing I needed when I went through some tough times in my marriage. I felt so alone. The first mistake was telling my story to anyone who would listen. God wanted me to talk to Him about my hurt and pain. He wanted me to tell Him how I cried, what was fair, what was not fair. God longs to hear from you wives. He wanted me to tell him what was on my heart and why it was hard for me to forgive others. I needed God to heal my whole heart.

We are equipped with every tool we need to run this race called marriage. Just look deep within yourself, it is there. Call upon God for whatever you need. I guarantee you that He who called you is faithful, and He will supply all your needs.

Wives, please connect with another wife who can mentor you and hold you accountable. Stay close to God and He will stay close to you. Most importantly, God will tell you how to meet your spouse needs.

The Gift of Servitude

Do you have the gift of servitude? Do you love serving others? Jesus came to serve, not be served. Remember when Jesus washed the feet of His disciples? Well, one of His disciples, Peter did not feel worthy of such an act. Jesus said, "sit down I am going to wash your feet." Can you imagine feeling unworthy of such an act? After all, this is the Messiah, Jesus! The Lamb of God who takes away all our sins. Even John the Baptist said, "I am unworthy to tie your sandal strap." Jesus said, "if you want to impress me, the first shall be last and the last shall be first."

John 1:27

Matthew 20:16

One of my gifts is servitude. During the holidays, I could remember, since I was a little girl, that I would love making plates to serve my family. I was so excited serving that I was always the last one at the table eating. My heart was filled with so much joy when I served others. Even today, my family members always ask me to make them a plate. I began to look for other ways to serve.

At my old church, I started serving on a Scholarship Ministry Board, which raised funds for college students. This ministry served at birthday parties, baby showers, graduation parties, and repasses. I served with great joy and I love to comfort others through the serving.

1 Corinthians 12:7-10

We all are given gifts and talents to use for God's glory. My husband has different gifts, (i.e. Wisdom, teaching, and healing hands). I used to tell him that he is wise beyond his years. This man always has warm hands too. I had foot surgery and there is something about his hands that it would calm the nerves down in my foot. Also, my husband loves to teach in his trade HVAC. I just want everyone to know that we all have been blessed with many gifts and talents to advance the Kingdom of God. We should not allow these gifts to lay dormant in us. You do not want to lose a good thing, especially if it was given to you by the Holy Spirit Himself.

Take Your Power Back

Taking your power back can be easier said than done. Sometimes, I think if I just hold on to my peace, I can get through this ordeal. How many of us know that it does not always pan out that way? You never know when God is assessing you for a promotion in Him, therefore, be alert.

For me, it is hard to be friends with people who have betrayed my trust. I decided to share a little of my testimony with someone who decided to spread that information to others in our circle of friends. To betray one's trust hurts, but we must forgive, do not hold on to that anger because that person will eventually hang themselves.

Isaiah 23:22

A lot of things that we do, we bring on ourselves. We have spoken words into the atmosphere, we have acted upon a sinful act, or thought that we were protecting ourselves from getting hurt again. The bible says, "The heart is deceitful above all things" and the issues of life flow from it. Also, the bible says, "In our tongue lies life or death, but to choose life so that we may live."

Jeremiah 17:9

I want to talk about taking your power back from the devil. Know that he uses the same road map each time on the people of God to trip us up so that we will fall. The devil's attacks are always the same, but the method may change. In other words, he uses who he can, when he can, and he makes the situation seem so bad that you will not even pray. Wives, we must pray without ceasing and remember that there is nothing uncommon to man that we should feel unworthy and not seek God in prayer.

1 Corinthians 10:13

God is the same today, yesterday, and forevermore; He does not change, but His methods of blessing will change. God does not change or move, we do. He is not a liar or the son of man that He shall repent. The Lord loves us with an everlasting heart. There is nothing that we can do that will separate us from the love of God. Do you know that God is no respecter of persons? He creates and loves us all the same.

Psalms 36:5-7

Ephesians 3:18

Obligated or Commanded

In marriage as a spouse, we are not obligated to do anything. I wrestled in my mind with what is a husband and wife's role in the marriage. The Holy Spirit began to deal with my heart concerning this matter. My expectations of a husband were worldly. My perspective of a marriage was based on a worldly view and I had to get rid of my unmet expectations.

A husband is commanded to love his wife as Jesus loves the church. The wife is commanded to respect her husband. These commands were given to us for specific reasons, (1) to follow Jesus's example, (2) to be obedient, and (3) to wash our minds with the water which is the Word. In other words, we need to renew our minds daily. Now, you see we are not obligated to do anything, but we are commanded to do things by the Holy Spirit.

Ephesians 5:21-33

I read a devotion that was titled, "A Monk Marriage," we are to be married with a thankful heart and be grateful for what we have before God can give us more. In marriage, we are not obligated, but we are "commanded" If your spouse is not walking in righteousness (the way of the Lord), then your spouse is either not ready to do so or has not received the gift of salvation.

Proverbs 21:3

We put a great burden on our spouses by expecting them to be everything to us. You first must be everything to God, yourself, and then others. Only Jesus can truly meet our every need. He is our happiness, peace, joy, healer, protector, provider, judge, and so much more. Jesus is our everything!

Jeremiah 29:11

Jesus meets all our needs according to His riches and glory in heaven. He alone heals, delivers, and sets His people free. Jesus meets our needs emotionally, intimately, and relationally. We must pray to God and ask Him for what we want to see more of in our spouses.

I do not know about you, but I have come too far to turn back now. We must go on to see what the end is going to be. As husbands and wives, we must change our mindsets, and develop a thankful heart. Begin to jot down in your journals at least one thing that you are thankful for each day and watch God change your perspective towards your spouse. Do not stop thanking God, this is an ongoing process.

Sacrifice or Obedience

What started out as a conversation between my husband and I, soon turned into a heated argument. I just wanted to get an understanding as to whether or not we wanted to continue in our marriage. My husband was stating what he gave up to be with me and I was merely stating what I went through to stay with him. We both have truly sacrificed something to be with each other.

The sacrificial lamb was slaughtered on the cross over 2000 years ago, our Lord and Savior, Jesus Christ. I heard this still small voice ask me, "What have you sacrificed for me?" Thinking to myself, I said, "I sacrificed my happiness, trust, and love to stay with your son because of my covenant with you Lord." Please know that we all are like sheep going to the slaughterhouse all day long.

To be true disciples, we must pick up our cross and follow Jesus. Our characters should look like and respond like Jesus. He never said a mumbling word as insults were hurled at Him, people spat on Him, they punched Him in the eye, whipped Him many times, and His side was pierced with a sword. When we think of our sacrifice, it will never top what Jesus endured on the cross for us.

Is it better for obedience or sacrifice? The Lord said, in His word that we will be rewarded openly for our obedience. Do you believe that? Jesus requires our obedience. When we obey His word, Jesus rewards us. He supplies all our needs, according to His riches and glory. Also, the favor of God rests upon us when we are obedient.

I have learned when we are obedient opposition will come, but if we stay the course, Jesus helps us and show us how much He loves us. Did you ever receive something you did not deserve, but because you were obedient, Jesus gave you exceedingly, abundantly above all that you could have asked for? Jesus will blow your mind.

I have learned in His Word, that Jesus requires obedience more than sacrifice. Jesus says, worry about you and do your part because He will do His part. He said, "Love your husband. I will help you to understand your husband and I will restore all."

1 Peter 2:23

1 Samuel 15: 22

Ephesians 3:20-21

Romans 12:2

Falling in Love versus Walking in Love

Do you remember when you first started dating your spouse? You were up all night talking on the phone and knew you had to get up for work the next morning. Remember when you loved everything about him or her; your spouse could do no wrong. Taking long walks through the park. Going to the movies and sharing a bucket of popcorn; those were the good old days.

You say to yourself, "I want to spend the rest of my life with this person." Now that you are married, you are like, "what was I thinking? How did this happen? Why didn't I see this coming?" I have one thing to say, "Love is blind." When you are in the in-love stage, nothing matters! You are in love and on cloud nine. Next is the reality stage, where the blinders come off and you both see each other for who you really are, who knew?

One day, I was mad at my husband because I had a bad day and he did not care enough to cater to my anger. All I wanted was for my husband to say, "It's going to be all right." He kept distancing himself from me because I had a stinky attitude which later escalated into hatred and then resentment. I was literally having a silent temper tantrum and the devil was working on my mind. How many people know that the devil is a liar? Instead of being mad at the situation God took me through, I was mad at my husband because he did not let my storm affect him.

Ephesians 4:31

At some point you must repent of your bad behavior and begin to speak over your life and bind up these evil spirits. You must know that you have power and authority over the enemy, and you are a child of God. We can be frustrated and get very depressed about a situation, but we need to know that God is in full control and He is the only one who can turn things around for us.

If one spouse is going through something, the other spouse should be there for love and moral support. This will help to bring the other spouse out of the mental and emotional state they are in. To walk in love is to ask your spouse, "Is everything okay? Is there anything that I can do for you?" Now, if your spouse is not ready to talk, please do not push, but wait until they are comfortable enough to talk about what happened.

Until we make a choice to walk in love, we will struggle in our relationships, especially our relationship with God. He loves us with all our flaws. He sees the best in us, therefore, if you are looking at the worst in each other, your marriage becomes stale and will not grow. My marriage was like a car stuck in the mud, and no matter what we did, we could not get it to move. Love is the antidote to every bad and evil thing in your life as it covers a multitude of sins.

1 Peter 4:8

When we make a choice to love, we are being the best that we can be for Jesus to use us. To God be the glory! We were created to worship the Lord, give Him all the glory, honor, and praise because He deserves it. God gave us His only begotten son, so that we will have everlasting life. To be mature in God, is to choose to walk in love.

Luke 10:27

Anger Management

I found myself at the Post Office signing for a certified letter in which I was skeptical about at first. The Police Abandonment Unit in my city was bringing a charge against me for my old vehicle that was not handled properly.

Can you imagine something you thought was over and done with comes back to bite you in the butt from a year ago. I had to go to Traffic Court, for an abandon vehicle that was found sitting on the street for a year. Well, it was my Nissan Pathfinder, oh how I loved this SUV. The engine and transmission both went at the same time leaving me no choice but to junk my jeep. I had a salvage company pick it up and in turn they gave me $350 in cash.

The Parking Authority representative suggested that I track down the salvage company to see if they would give me a copy of the receipt. Yes, you guessed it, I could not find my receipt because I left the matter in my husband's hands and went to work that day. All I kept thinking was, this was a year ago, and how can I track down that receipt.

They gave my husband and I, the run around for days, stating that they could not find it, or that the owner was away and that we had to wait for him to return. Finally, they gave us a new receipt with $300 in cash money. I thought cool, I can go online to pay the ticket in which I did, but to my surprise, there were two more tickets totaling $700. I was really pissed off. I called PPA again and the representative suggested for me to go to court with all my documentations and receipts so that they can clear these tickets out of the system.

I believed the representative and went into the Traffic Court with confidence that I was going to be cleared of all charges. How many people know that this almost never happens? I sat for two hours just to see a court representative who explained to me that I had been misinformed! My heart sank in my chest. Instead of walking out of there with a clean slate, they sent me next door to make payment arrangements.

I was so angry that things did not turn out in my favor that I could not see God working on my behalf. I believe what the Parking Authority representative said, about wiping those tickets out of the system. I thought this is not my fault.

God began to deal with me. He said, "Put your trust in me because people will fail you every time." God told me that I should have taken off that day to handle my own car issue instead of leaving everything for my husband to handle as the vehicle was in my name, thus holding me responsible. He, also, told me it was Him who got me the low $26 monthly installment payments for a year. Instead of being mad, I should have been thankful that it was not bad. Here are a few scriptures that helped me to persevere through and get my anger under control.

Ephesians 4:26

Ephesians 4:22-32

Psalm 146:3-7

Romans 12:2

Being angry does not produce the righteousness of God, therefore, it does not produce any fruit. The bible says, "To put off every weight that beseeches you." Also, get rid of all rage, malice, bitterness, and any other evil intent. To carry this bad fruit is a blessing blocker. God cannot answer your prayers.

Temptations in the Marriage

There are many temptations that are hurled at us all day long. How do you handle temptations? What tempts you the most? We have all been there. God knows our weaknesses and so does the devil. The Lord tempts no one.

When my husband lost his job due to a motor vehicle accident while on a job assignment in Ohio, which put him out of work for a while. I said, "For better or worse, I'm going to take care of my husband." I worked, and he had some income coming in, but it stopped. The marriage suffered a financial setback.

My husband was stripped of his job, he lost a couple of vehicles, and not to mention it, he was grieving the loss of his grandmother. He became an angry and very depressed man. Nothing I did seem to help. We argued all the time about money, and he would tell me that I needed to be more affectionate. As a wife, I thought I was doing all the right things.

I was tempted to walk away from my marriage a few times. There was a period of two years and a half that my husband was not working. I was working full-time, taking online courses, and was just tired, which left little time for my husband. As a wife, you naturally want to step in and help, but God does not need our help, he needs us to trust him. I started praying for restoration in my marriage and standing on God's promises.

Through many trials and temptations, I grew closer to God. I learned that my job was to get on my knees and pray. God strengthened me, gave me compassion, and a deeper love for my husband. He removed people and things out of our lives. God showed us that we were stronger together than we were apart. He taught us how to meet each other needs; we are still a work in progress. My husband now has a city job. I know that there is nothing impossible for God.

We are tempted all day long, believe it or not, this is Satan's strategy to get the believer to doubt God. Knowing who you are in Christ helps you to defeat Satan. Being obedient and trusting God to fix your situation helps, but as a believer you must do your part. Nothing is impossible for God.

Do you want to be free? Stop falling for the same traps and make the choice today to be obedient. Let God strengthen you and prepare your hands for war and give you a promise for your marriage to stand on until it manifests in your life. We must choose to always trust God and walk by faith and not by sight.

Deuteronomy 30:15-20

Forgiveness

Forgiveness is for you, not the other person. The bible says, forgive and forgive as often as God forgives you. We imprison ourselves when we don't forgive, and we allow the person who has hurt us to have power over us.

We need to simply let go and let God. Letting go gives you freedom and a remarkable amount of peace. The bible says, "Those who are free in Jesus are free indeed." Where Jesus is, there is liberty. Quickly letting go of the offense as soon as it arrives helps you to be a better person.

Colossians 3:13

To carry unforgiveness is like walking around with a very heavy backpack of bricks (offenses) everywhere you go. God says, "Cast your cares upon me, for I care for you." He also said, "My burdens are light, and my yoke is easy, come learn of me."

Sometimes when we harbor unforgiveness and we will not let the situation go, God must sit us down. For instance, you may be laid-off from work and finding a new job may seem impossible. Interviews may come, they may go, and it may seem like you are being punished. God is simply saying, you are not ready. He is concerned about the condition of your heart and mind.

Jesus also, cares about how you treat others. How can you love a God whom you cannot see, but you hate your brother whom you do see? We need to care enough to get it right with others which will cause us to walk in right relationship with God.

Ephesians 4:32

When you harbor unforgiveness, it blocks your prayers from being heard by God. In other words, it is a blessing blocker and you are not growing spiritually. God loves to bless his children. The bible says, there is no good thing that He will withhold from his children.

Harden not your hearts for your attitude really does determine your altitude. Behavior that is out of control, keeps us out of the will of God. I remember God asking me, "My daughter don't you want to dine at my table?" And I began to cry. John the Baptist, talked about repenting, we need to confess our sins to one another, repent so Jesus can hear from heaven and heal our land.

Hebrews 3:15

"Get right or get left," I love this metaphor because if we do not get right with others then we cannot get right with God. We will get to the pearly white gates and Jesus is going to say, "Depart from me, for I do not know you."

While we did not deserve it, Jesus died on the cross for our sins. Why not show that same grace and mercy towards others by forgiving as often as God forgives you, even though they may not deserve it. To tell you the truth, none of us are deserving. To God be the glory!

Provider

How are you providing for your significant other? I walked in the door of my mother's house and my younger brother was complaining to my cousin, Paul about how much he provides for his girlfriend and the fact that he does not get any credit for it. We should serve one another, not looking for anything in return.

Being a provider financially is just one of the things a woman needs. Ultimately, she needs your general concern, your listening ears, for you to not only love her, but to affirm her and restore what is broken in her. A woman needs conversation. Why do you think Eve was talking to the serpent in the garden? She probably said, "Adam isn't talking to me and besides, what the serpent is saying sounds so amazing right now."

To all the men and women across the globe, if you are giving your money and no emotional, moral support, or communication, you are only doing half the job. Learn your spouse's love language, there are five of them: Quality time, Affirmation, Gifts, Physical Touch, and Acts of Service. Once you do this, it makes your home and family life run so much smoother.

A man can open his wallet all he wants, but money cannot buy a woman's love. Do you meet her physical, spiritual, emotional, and psychological needs? Do you ask her how she is feeling today? How was her day at work? Is there anything in her heart that she would like to talk about?

A woman has needs just like a man. When you meet her deepest needs, she will feel a sense of security, then she will blossom like the beautiful flower she is supposed to be. She will truly open her heart up to you without worrying about if you will hurt her. A woman needs to be able to be vulnerable with her husband and yet still be sexy and sensuous. We do not want to be hard like men.

When women have truly opened their hearts up to love, they will do this with the thought "if I'm hurt, I will forgive." I know firsthand that God will bring healing to all those who are hurting. We got to give our hurts and pains over to God so that He can heal us. Carrying it around is not good. Remember, love covers a multitude of sins.

Ephesians 4:32

1 Peter 5:7

1 Peter 4:8

Put Jesus Back on the Throne

Is Jesus on the throne of your heart or your spouse? I worried so much about my marriage that I heard the Holy Spirit say, "Take your spouse off the throne." He was so right. I made my circumstances in my marriage bigger than my God. There were many days that I consumed myself with worrying thoughts about my marriage.

We must learn not to put any other gods or idols before our Lord and Savior, Jesus Christ. Here is where we get in trouble. Satan likes to use the fear tactic all the time. If you fear that this or that is going to happen then most likely it will because with your thoughts, you are speaking a thing into existence just by what you believe. Do you know that we sin against Jesus in our thought process? We need to renew our minds daily by the washing of the word.

Listen, my husband and I had stopped being intimate simply because our work schedules were different, we were just too tired. One spouse wasn't trying to meet the other spouse halfway. We always talked about compromise, but it never seemed to happen on our terms, but God. As wives and husbands, we got to make time for each other, it is imperative that we do or suffer the consequences of God's wrath.

Sexual intimacy is a form of worship created by God himself. I read an article that sexual intimacy gives birth to something or grows something existing (his/her love for you). Did you know that a marriage without sex is offensive to the Lord? Sex is more than pleasuring your spouse, it is a form of worship ladies and gentlemen. We have got to do marriage one way, God's way. Wives we must look at sex through the eyes of God or we will continue to think it is a chore.

Genesis 2:22

Ephesians 5:28-29

1 Corinthians 7:5

Ephesians 4:26

1 Peter 5:8

Sustainability

I love the song by Koryn Hawthorne, "Won't He Do It." The Lord will sustain you through good and bad times. Our minds are prone to remembering the bad times and the feelings associated with those moments in life.

For a long time, I hated hanging pictures on the wall or taking pictures, especially if it reminded me of a bad time in my life. I just did not want to be reminded of the pain. How many of us know that God will bring you back to that moment in time to remind you that He was right there with you keeping you through it all. We cannot dismiss or wipe out of our memories, the fact that God was there, and if it were not for God on our side where would we be?

The Lord said to Paul, "My Grace is sufficient," and He is saying the same thing to us today. The Lord is the same yesterday, today, and forevermore; He changes not. The Lord wants us to tell our stories, so what is your testimony? Your testimony will not only save other lives, but it will free you to be whole in Jesus Christ.

2 Corinthians 12:9

I am reminded of many characters in the Bible who lived to write the stories that we read today. Not only did David, Luke, John, Esther, and so many others tell their stories, but they were witnesses to God's goodness and found it not robbery to write about the goodness of the Lord.

Paul said, I knew what it was to be hungry and to feast. He knew what is was to receive forty lashes across his back and to be healed. I knew what it was to struggle with domestic abuse, physically and mentally in my early twenties and to get out after five years. I, also, struggled with the fear of looking over my shoulders for many years after the abuse to living in complete freedom today. I know what it means to have low self-esteem (the worldly view of myself) and to have high self-esteem (which is wrapped up in everything that I am in Jesus- the heavenly view of myself).

Philippians 4:12-13

Knowing who you are in Christ is your total identity. Only the Lord holds the blueprint of your life destiny in his hands. Jesus is a man who told me everything about my life. You see, I was the woman at the well seeking for the type of water where I will never thirst again. One drink is all you need, and you will never forget all the wonderful things that the Lord has done and will continue to do for you.

Spiritual Maturity

I went to church one Sunday morning and the preacher was talking about how we are a microwave generation that wants God to act immediately. He stated, "We pray and ask God for something, but we immediately get up to leave without waiting for the answer." I was angry when I heard this message because it was the truth.

I prayed, but I did not allow God to speak to me about my circumstances. It was like, I was talking to God, got up from praying, and left without waiting for an answer. God wants us to mature in Him. One day, I finally stuck around after prayer to hear what God had to say.

It turns out, that God is concerned about everything that concerns me. He wants a relationship with us. He longs to talk, laugh, and cry with us. Did you know that your marriage relationship is a representation of your relationship with God? I was turning my back on God and my husband was walking away from me when I wanted to talk. My God!

- Cast your cares upon me, for I care for you (Luke 12:22-26)
- He will contend with those who contend with you (Isaiah 49:25)
- He will comfort you (Psalm 119:7) ()
- He will heal you (Isaiah 57:18)
- He will provide for you (Genesis 22:14)
- When I was a child… (1 Corinthians 13:11)

If He said it, then it will be done. I believe we walk away thinking, "Maybe He will and maybe He will not answer." People, we have got to have more faith than that. For our hope is built on nothing less than Jesus Christ's righteousness. There is no good thing that He will withhold from His children. We are children of "The Most-High God," we are heirs to the throne, and we share in the inheritance in Jesus Christ.

Rejection Builds Character

If anyone knows what rejection feels like or even looks like it is our Lord and Savior, Jesus Christ firsthand. He was God in the flesh and the only perfect man that ever walked this earth.

You may have experienced rejection throughout various times in your life and it can be very hurtful even to the point of devastation. To me, rejection feels like punishment. No one likes to be rejected. I had to learn that God is the only perfect man who ever walked this earth. If man rejects me, it is not the end of the world. Putting your trust in man will fail you every time.

God loves us and accepts us with an everlasting love. We set our hope on Jesus who is the everlasting God. Set your hope on love who is God Almighty Himself. I will remain confident in this that I will see the goodness of the Lord before I leave this earth. You see, God just wants to strengthen us.

Rejection of marriage hurts because you do not expect it to come from the one whom you love. While, I was lying in bed, I happen to hear Author, Lysa TurKeurst speak about rejection on the Trinity Broadcast Network (TBN). She said, "She did two years of research on "Rejection" alone before she wrote her book, "It's Not Supposed to Be This Way." Lisa is a wonderful author who broke down the meaning of rejection. She talked about how the rejection facts and the impact of those facts can affect a person's life greatly.

God wants us to extract from the facts to get an understanding. For instance, rejection means to be excluded from something and sometimes without cause. Instead of us walking away with this reality, we take things to heart, and dwell on the "Why?" Do not get so caught up on the "Why," but understand that God's timing is perfect and will not delay.

The Lord wants to teach us something when we are going through these tough times in our lives. He wants us to endure and persevere through it, so that we will come out looking more and more like His son, Jesus Christ. He is literally trying to burn some worldly view out of us and give us his view on life. God wants to mode us into the character of His son, Jesus. Why would you not want to be more like Christ?

Romans 12:15

Psalm 119:50

Psalm 34:18

Remember:

- You are not picked on by God, but you have been chosen before the foundations of the earth.
- God sees the beauty in suffering which represents a light, His Glory (the glory of God).
- There is beauty in your brokenness, for God is near the broken hearted.
- You are beautifully and wonderfully made in the image of God.
- You are a child of "The Most-High God", a child of righteousness.

Pain Is A Teacher

There is something about pain that puts a fire under our feet and gets us going in the right direction. I do not know about you, but I hate any type of pain that makes me uncomfortable. If I have any pain, I quickly want a cure for it. Our Lord and Savior uses pain which afterwards brings about His great reveal.

We go through fiery trials to come out looking like pure gold. Our trials teach us about ourselves, God, and others. Trials are painful and will urge us to change our mindsets thus changing the misbehavior to move on to the next level in God. If we did not go through something painful, we will never connect with God. We cannot get too comfortable where we are because, like Jesus, we move from glory to glory.

Pain is the only thing that will teach us a valuable lesson, but it also gives us a gift of not making that painful mistake again. Our testimonies are to help others by giving them hope in Jesus. To testify of God's goodness and how He brought you out causes you to remember the pain and impart knowledge on to others so that they will not make the same mistake.

Knowing that we have a sweet victory in God, why not rejoice in times of trouble? I used to think that rejoicing while feeling hurt, discouraged, rejected, disappointed, and so much more was impossible. One day, I heard a sermon preached called "Rejoice for What?" And it gave me a new perspective. The pain is an indication that God is trying to get something to you and me such as a gift, a talent, valuable information, etc. We get mad because we do not know what is going on, but we ought to rejoice and trust God in whatever he is doing.

Our Heavenly Father just wants to bless us abundantly. We should not get but rejoice in the Lord. Did you know that your praise confuses the enemy? The one thing that I have learned, when I do not feel like praying or rejoicing in the Lord is the time to turn on my praise music. The music moves in my heart and allows me to praise the Lord. I feel so much better afterwards, it puts a smile not only on my face, and it leaves an imprint on my heart.

Philippians 4:4-8

2 Samuel 6:14-16

Fear

The meaning of fear is an unpleasant emotion caused by the belief that someone or something dangerous, likely to cause pain, or a threat. Fear holds you back from doing what it is that God has called you to do.

I learned my lesson the hard way by operating out of fear. Please hear my heart, this is not good. Doing things out of fear is just you trying to protect you. Basically, God does not need your help protecting you.

- Fear causes you to be afraid and back up.
- Fear is the culprit behind the rejection.
- Fear is the culprit behind pride.
- Fear will cause you to react out of your feelings.
- Fear will cause you to lose out on life and God's blessings.
- Fear will cause you to be paralyzed in some areas of life.
- Fear will allow you to talk yourself out of a blessing.
- Fear will keep you going in cycles until you decide to come out.

I learned that becoming complacent at times is not always good because we get too comfortable. For many of us, we do not like change. We do not like deviating from our normal schedules.

For me, I hated being inconvenienced. God is saying, can I use you for a minute, hour, or a day? We vision in our minds, the outcome of things, and talk our way out of our destiny which allows us to stay in our comfort zone. Our comfort zone most times, causing us to miss out on what God has for us.

People, you must be inconvenienced, if you want to serve the Lord. He is an unusual God, out of the box God, and nothing is impossible for God. The only one who can stop you is "You."

God has so much more for us if we just come out of our comfort zone. Stop using crutches to protect yourself from the realities of life (i.e. Comfort foods, alcohol, and drugs). The Bible did not say, "Get hurt, but to get an understanding." If you never move, you will never know all that God has for you.

In conclusion, fear is what you tell yourself in your mind. You must learn to silence the negative voices, which is you, and start speaking positive things over yourself. It is not enough to read the word, but you must live it out (practice it in your everyday life). Here are the scriptures that helped me:

Joshua 1:9

Isaiah 41:10

Psalm 56:3

John 14:27

1 John 4:18

Isaiah 43:1

Matthew 6:34

Psalm 27:1

Psalm 55:22

2 Timothy 1:7

Offended

Are you easily offended? Can you take criticism well? I must admit that I struggle in this area. People would say hurtful things to me, do stupid things to me, then I would shut down and be unresponsive for a couple of days. If you love me, I just believe that you would not do anything to hurt me. Ladies and gentlemen, our love ones are the very ones who will hurt/offend us several times a day. For we are sheep going to the slaughterhouse all day long.

It is easy to be offended, especially, if it is something that has not yet been addressed with your spouse that lingers. The enemy knows just how to tempt us in this area. If we are tired, hungry, or agitated he comes in like a flood. God says, "When the enemy comes in like a flood, I will raise up a standard against him," and He always keeps His word. God watches over His word to perform it in our lives.

To get over an offense, we must forgive it quickly and ask God to heal our hearts and emotions. Here is an area that is a struggle for me, but God. He said forgive as often as I have forgiven you. We must release people from the prison of unforgiveness less God forgives us. Paul says, "I press on towards the goal in Christ Jesus," thus closing the door on unforgiveness.

Proverbs 4:23

Matthew 18:21-22

Psalms 119:165

God wants us to have loving relationships. He wants us to get our relationships right with our spouses and then bring our offering to the alter. When we do not forgive others and turn them over to God, more offenses come. God is giving us an opportunity to turn it over to Him. When we don't trust God, we are being prideful, and are showing God that we have a better plan.

All things are better left in the hands of God. He says, "For my burdens are light and my yoke is easy, come learn of me." Ladies and gentlemen, we do not have to receive the offense, therefore, when it comes you can simply say, "I don't receive it," then plead the blood of Jesus against it. See, we really do have a choice.

Offenses can be stumbling blocks for us if we do not deal with it immediately in our lives. Know that you are a child of The Most-High God and a child of righteousness. We all fall short of the glory of God each day, but because Christ got up with all power in His hands we can too. Remember, being angry does not produce the righteousness of God and it hinders our prayers.

Familiarity I

We all have favorite places, people, and things that we love to return to. You know how you have a familiar way of doing a thing and it is always worked for you in the past, well it will not anymore.

For me, I love going back home for the holidays to enjoy family, food, and fun. Getting to share the holidays with loved ones is important to me. Now, that I am married and have a family of my own, I noticed that my extended family does not get together as much around the holidays.

My sisters and I would help mom to make a huge dinner for Thanksgiving and Christmas. We always had a huge turkey, ham, rabbit, baked macaroni and cheese, greens, potato salad, and do not forget sweet potato and apple pie. All the family would meet at mom's house and we would have a wonderful time. It is hard getting folks all together under one roof. The excuses start to ring out. The Lord said, "Daphney, you are the one still holding to old traditions." I cannot help it, I love my family, and those traditions.

Gravitating to the familiar is holding on to the old way or the process of doing something. For me it always has to do with my childhood, in dreams, I always find myself back home in the house I grew up in. I have always held on hold to my family traditions, but God is saying, "It's time to start your own." My daughter tried to tell me, but I just did not want to accept the truth.

We tend to do the same thing when it comes to trials and tribulations of going back to the familiar and what always worked in the past. Know that God's method of deliverance and victory will change each season of our lives. Do not look for God to do the same thing the same way each time. We must trust and listen to his still yet small voice within us to guide and lead us into all truth.

1 Kings 19:11-13

Isaiah 43:19

2 Corinthians 5:17

Matthew 9:17

If you are anything like me, I always go back to what is safe and familiar. I realize, now that I am older that God does not want us to go back to what we are used to. He wants you and me to truly rely on Him. Trusting fully in God is what is going to propel us forward in life.

Hanging around familiar places and people will keep you stuck, and you will learn eventually that you got to move on. God changes from glory to glory and because His spirit is within us, we too must move. We must get out of our comfort zone and contentment to move forward.

God, break the chain of familiarity, in Jesus' name. I bind the familiar spirits in the name of Jesus that keep us stuck so that we will not go to the next level with you- God, in Jesus name, Amen. Each level in God builds our character and helps shape us into who God has called us to be.

Familiarity II

We love to hold on to people, places, and things that are familiar in other words because it feels safe with us. When my granddaughter was in the first grade, she was learning about nouns which are person, places, or things. Why do you think that is? Because our memory retains information based on persons, places, things. Let us talk about looking back, when to move forward, and letting go of the past/familiar.

Reasons not to look back:

- You cannot change the past
- You are not the same person you were back then
- God cannot give you new opportunities
- It is a waste of your time

Reasons to look back:

- Remind yourself how far you have come and thank God
- It is good to reflect on the good and loving memories of your life
- Remind yourself of your mission to set forth goals
- To learn from the negative cycles in your life

We all need to learn from the negative life cycles and break generational curses that has been passed on to us. The sins of the parents really do fall on the children, but because you are sealed with God's Holy Spirit (the Promise) you have the power to be a game changer (ambassador for Christ). You will change life cycles for generations to come.

Here are some generational cycles we need to break, (i.e. That person is not good for me, this place causes me to drink and party like its 1999, this food causes my Diabetes and Hypertension to rise, therefore, I need to change). Come on, we got to be real with ourselves people. God does not want us to go back when He brings us out of something. Godly wives, mercy brings us out of bad situations, therefore, trust God and do not go back. Looking back is a temptation and you reject God when you fall for that fleshly desire. God can no longer help a frustrated woman, if you are going to keep falling for the same temptation every time.

2 Timothy 4:10

1 Kings 13:4

John 6:60-66

By faith, we got to put some stuff into practice in our lives. Please know that as a believer you are going to be tempted to go back. Satin is just doing his job, but when will we do our jobs to advance the Kingdom of God? For your sake, I hope you are not tempted to walk away when it gets tough. Jesus will never leave us or forsake us.

As a dog returns to his vomit, so makes a fool to his foolishness. There is nothing good in it, some people might say, "What a stupid dog. That is so disgusting." God is not in it! Our nasty sins, in fact, those sins were nailed to the cross over 2000 years ago. Backsliding only gets worse for the believer. Jesus is married to the backslider.

To know this, a nasty sin habit that a believer must break is important so that it is not passed on to our children and grandchildren. If your house is not clean, that spirit comes back with seven more spirits stronger. Do not be a backslider by looking back. Lot's wife looked back and became a pillar of salt. Jesus moves from glory to glory. He is not in your circumstances.

Proverbs 26:11

Luke 9:62

Pride in Marriage

Having pride is bad for us all because this stands in the way of us loving one another properly. Let us discover what it really means to be prideful. Being prideful means that a person is arrogant and disdainful; one who thinks highly of themselves.

Prideful people do not have a lot of friends in their circle. They tend to think they are on a higher level than everyone else and they simply cannot be touched. These people are also loaners, leaders that cannot be followers, and can be very antisocial because they think they do not need correction. How can we be antisocial when we serve a social God?

Jesus associated with all walks of life in the bible, (i.e. Tax collector, adulterer, murderer, liar, prostitute, etc.). He loves His people because He created us with love and family in mind. The bible says that He predestined us before the foundations of the earth. Jesus will never leave us or forsake us.

A prideful person thinks their way is perfect, and that you should follow them as a God. After all, they think they have the best solutions to problems. We all have pride in us, but it must die. Now let us not get pride confused with confidence in ourselves! We should be confident in all that we do and do it with excellence (i.e. One who is confident in how they do their work, confident in raising responsible children, and confident in how they live their life for God).

When you think you can do something better than your spouse, or shall I say compete with your spouse, that is pride in your heart. Do not get mad at your spouse because he/she does things differently or even better than you. God puts two people together from two totally different upbringings to maximize their capacity to love like Him. We come to the altar with all our baggage from childhood to adulthood; do not act like you are free of baggage.

The bible says, "Pride comes before a fall." Do not let your pride lead you off into a ditch with other fellow pigs. Have you ever heard of the, "Blind leading the Blind?"

Husbands in marriage, need to put their pride aside for the sake of the family. He must provide and protect his family regardless of what issues he might have with that family member. Christ is the head of the husband and the husband is the head of the wife. For your marriage to be successful, it needs to be built on a firm foundation.

I remember the Holy Spirit is saying to me, your husband does not have to do things your way, as your way is not perfect. Jesus is the only perfect man who has ever walked this earth. There are seven sins, Jesus hates: Lust, envy, anger, greed, gluttony, slothfulness, and of course pride.

Proverbs 6:16-19

Romans 12:3

1 Timothy 6:9-10

Colossians 4:5

Romans 12:19

Proverbs 14:30

Proverbs 16:32

Proverbs 25:28

Let it Go

There is this App called, "Let Go," where you can post a picture of the item you would like to let go for a cost. Now, the asking price is all up to you.

People tend to hold on to old antiques, clothes that are too small, a favorite couch or love seat, but this App allows you to let go of an item you would not normally part with no matter what. Putting a price on something that has sentimental value seems hard to do, but you know deep down inside you must let go.

God is saying, "You must release something in your hand/possession first to be blessed." Do you have something that you would like to let go (i.e. Attitude, negativity, hurt, pain, old belongings, furniture, car, etc.)? Well, this is the year of blessings. I can hear God saying, "Test me and see that I will pour you out a blessing, that there will not be room enough to contain it."

Ecclesiastes 3:6

Ephesians 4:31-32

Hebrews 12

For me, the hardest thing to let go was the past hurt and pain of an abusive relationship. All though you have grown up, moved away, those memories are still there. One day, boom out of nowhere, I see this person walking down the street, and those old feelings come back like it was yesterday, the fourth of July fireworks. When this happens, it is because all though time has passed, you have been holding onto the offense, the hurt, and all the pain associated with it for years. For some of you this may not be your story, but I am sure there is something you need to let go.

A lot of us are walking around with gaping wounds that are bleeding out. Remember the woman with the issue of blood in the bible. Doctors could not even heal this woman. She knew she had to get to Jesus! One touch of the hem of His garment and she became whole. I believe she put her pride and issues aside and was willing to crawl on her knees to get to Jesus. Now, that is a determined woman. Do you want to be made whole again? Who does not want to be blessed?

It is time to let it go, says God. Truly, trust Him with your pain and hurt. "For all things work together for the good of those that love God and are called according to His purpose." Ladies and Gentlemen, it does not get no better than this. God says, "I want to take you to higher heights in Me (new levels in God)." Fix your focus, do not let it be on your circumstances, but put it on Jesus and where He desires to take you.

Today, I let it go! I want to live my best life, living in peace with everyone. I do not want to hold onto things that will hinder my blessings. You know, those things that do not bear fruit in my life.

Philippians 3:13-14

Proverbs 4:25-27

Philippians 4:8-9

Love Covers a Multitude of Sins

God is love and love is God. According to 1 Corinthians 13, Love is the only thing that will last. Let us talk about why other person's sins are before us. For example, you see someone sin and you get mad because you do not know what to do or how you can help that person. You ask the Lord, "How can I pray for this person?" First, take your eyes off the wrong that they have done, because they sin differently from you.

Can I tell you, that is not our job or a place to do anything, God is saying, "Sit your arrogant, prideful, self-absorbed butt down somewhere?!" I showed you all of this because I want you to believe Me for a divine turn around in this person's life. We are not supposed to point out the way others sin, but we are to believe the promise God gave to you concerning that person.

Remember, Noah in the bible drank so much wine until he was knocked out sleep and naked. Noah's son saw this, laughed, and went to get his other two brothers to join in with him. Instead, they took a sheet, walked backwards into their father's tent, and covered his drunkenness/nakedness. Noah's two sons showed grace and mercy towards their father. That is the love which covers a multitude of sins.

Listen, Noah would have awakened in shame and most likely beat himself up more because of his drunken state being exposed to his children. I can imagine him falling deeper into his sin and drinking more to suppress the thought of someone knowing his shameful secret.

Our job is to trust God and take Him at His word. Jesus did not say lose sleep because you are taking the offense personal, but rest in knowing He will do just what He says He will do. Jesus watches over His word so that He will perform it. The Devil is trying to distract you to get you to curse yourself. He knows he cannot curse what God has blessed. Some of you can hear demonic spirits talking to you or about you. Know that these evil spirits are mad because you are on schedule and their job is to throw you off track. They are hanging around looking for a loophole, take that message back to their father, Satan, to devise a plan to get you to turn away from God.

Stay in the word which will keep your focus/faith in God, so when offenses come, they will bounce off you and you will move forward with the grace of God. Things that use to get you down and upset will not matter anymore because you have moved on. God is not in our circumstances. He is not in our past because He has left that place. I can hear God say, "Move on and persevere daughter/son because I have chosen you and equipped you with every tool for such a time as this."

Remember, Esther was taken against her will to the King's palace to become one of King Xerxes' concubines, but that was not it. Her cousin Mordecai says, "Who knows? Maybe you were put in this position for such a time as this to save the Jews, but if you do nothing, you too will perish." In other words, you have a job to do. You are responsible to cover others no matter if it means death for you. The King did not know Esther was a Jew, but she spoke up and God saved all the Jews. God will back you when you do your part.

1 Corinthians 13

Esther 2:8

Esther 2:20-22

Esther 4:4

No Lack

Believing that you must replenish your supply before it runs out can be a fear of yours. There is no lack in Jesus, therefore, there is no lack in you. The Lord will supply all our needs according to His riches and glory in Christ Jesus in heaven. I have learned that, sometimes buying more just so that you will not run out can hinder you from God's blessing. God said, "You have an orphan spirit," which means you do not believe that you have a heavenly father who will provide for you.

If your hands are full then God cannot replenish you. What you are saying is this, "I'm good Lord, see I got it." Did you know that if you can get it with your bank account, then God is not needed? God specializes in lost. He is near the broken hearted. God is the only one who can fill you up again. I remember when my husband was out of work and doing little odd jobs here and there. We were low on groceries and I was worrying how we were going to make it to the following week as most of my paycheck was going towards the mortgage and other bills.

I got down on my knees and reverence God and I told Him that there is no lack in Him. I asked God to help me with the meat order. He caused my husband to put cash money in my hand to go towards the groceries. God did it suddenly. I never worry about what to wear, eat, or anything anymore. Won't He do it!

I never doubt what God can do. If you have the right motives, whatever you ask for in Jesus' name, He will give unto you according to His will.

Psalm 23

Deuteronomy 2:7

Philippians 4:19

Stress

I am sitting and thinking about what I can tell a person who says that they are always stressed. God began to share with me that people who stress do so because they have a fear of loss. They have lost so much over the years that they do not want to lose one more thing in their lives.

When we are stressed, it is usually because we have had many losses, one after another in our lives. Can I just tell you that we are not to look at what we have lost, but what we have and be thankful? God does not want us looking back on what was no more, but to be grateful for what we have now.

I know that loosing loved ones can be very difficult for anyone, but remember that God will provide peace, comfort, and strength. I get that it is easier said than done, so have your moment. The key is not to get stuck there! We still must carry on with our lives as our loved ones would have wanted us to do. Just know that all we can do after our loved ones are gone is to keep their memories alive in our hearts, celebrate their life, and never forget them. Hopefully, we will see them again in heaven.

God does not want you to be depressed beloved. He wants you to be happy. In the bible, He says, "Choose this day whom you will serve," and "Choose life or death." We have free will which means we have a choice. I would surely hope that you choose life, for we shall live and not die.

There is are a couple of songs that I want to introduce you to if you have not heard them, by Travis Greene, "*Made A Way*" and "*Intentional.*" God is intentional and knows how many hairs that are on your head. He knows what you need before you even ask.

Our God loves us with an everlasting love and there is nothing that He will withhold from His children. There is nothing that is impossible for God. He moves mountains and calls walls to fall. He has the power to perform miracles in our lives. Godly wives, we are where we are today only because God made a way. Lord, we are so grateful for all of you and we thank you Jesus!

Prayer:

Lord, we bind up stress, depression, oppression, regression, and every evil demonic spirit that does not look like you. We lose the power of God in our lives to move mountains. Oh God, we thank you that you cause giants to fall. We are your sons and daughters and we call upon you to fight this battle on our behalf. Thank you, for moving every mountain, tearing down every stronghold that exalts itself up against the word of God, and your power is performing miracles. We thank you Oh God for what you are doing in our lives, for it is in Jesus' name we pray, Amen!

Dignity

The definition for 'Dignity' is the state or quality of being worthy of honor or respect. A composed or serious manner or style, and/or a sense of pride in oneself; self-respect.

The anger a person holds in their heart will be directed at the closest person to them. God is saying to them, "Come out of the cave, you've been in there for far too long. Who or what hurt you? You can't beat people down with your words anymore."

When one loses their dignity, he/she becomes lost. You find your dignity when you know your self-worth, respect yourself, and know who you are in Christ:

- You are the apple of God's eye (Psalms 17:8)
- You are a child of Righteousness (2 Corinthians 5:21)
- You are the head and not the tail (Deuteronomy 28:13)
- You are blessed and highly favored (Luke 1:28)
- You are healed, saved, and delivered (Jeremiah 17:14)

Getting your dignity back starts with you. Understand that you must see yourself the way that God sees you. Get rid of your stinking thinking and make sure that your behavior is in tune with who God called you to be. Do not worry about how others see you, because it really does not matter what they say. God has the final say. Understand that people will show you who they are, and your job is to believe them. Therefore, understand the intent verses the impact of a person's words. They can tell you the sky is blue, meaning they can tell you anything. Do not believe something you have not researched yourself.

Learn to be culturally aware because people do and say things based on their culture. Remember, you are taught about your culture during your childhood and it stays with you for life. Did you know that culture can be a behavior which is learned and passed down from generation to generation? This is exactly, why generational curses must be broken.

Try finding common ground with others. God commands us to love one another as He has first loved us. We are to love the person but hate the sin in them. Partner up with another believer and join your faith together, pray, and watch God work miracles in both of your lives. Do not be led into darkness, but you lead the way into the light. God called us to be leaders, come out from under those who want you to follow them. Choose God's way of leading.

Most importantly, even when our flesh wants to do wrong, do the right thing, because God will reward you for your obedience openly. Having dignity is having a quality of life and Jesus says, "Come unto me all who are heavy laden, and I will give you rest." Jesus' grace and mercy are new every day!

Unequally Yoked

What happens when you marry someone who does not share the same spiritual beliefs, and morals/values? I believe this discussion should take place before a couple decides to get married. To have a spiritual discussion in your home can sometimes become a debate. Men and women often have different views about their spiritual life, even if they are of the same faith.

What do you do when you are already married to an unbeliever? The believing spouse is to pray for the unbelieving spouse. As the believer you must continue to do what is right in the eyes of the Lord.

1 Corinthians 7:12-20

The Bible says, "You don't know wife/husband, when you will win your spouse over with your meek spirit." Wives we are to be quiet, everything does not require a response. Ladies, we need to submit to our husbands. Gentlemen, you are to love your wives as Jesus loves the church and gave Himself up for her.

Just want to share with you a few meanings for "Unequally Yoke":

- A yoke is a wooden bar that joins two oxen together so that they can pull the weight together.
- Not aligned with God's design for marriage.
- Not like minded- wisdom.
- Do not have the same morals/values.
- Not same in character/heart.
- Not on the same page with your spouse.

- Not moving in the same direction, thus not becoming one whole.

1 Peter 3:1-12

Amos 3:3

1 Corinthians 13

If your spouse is not walking in righteousness, your job is to pray that your spouse will take their rightful place (as head of household, husband, father, grandfather and wives, likewise, you as the center of household, wife, mother, grandmother). If you trust God, then you know that He will answer your prayer in His appointed time. Ask God to give you a promise for your marriage and stand on it until it manifests in your life.

Godly wives, trust God as He is not a man that He should lie or the son of man that He shall repent. Know that the marital relationship does not lose its sacredness if there is one believing spouse praying for God to shine His light in their spouses' heart.

Worship

To worship God is to express your reverence and adoration for Him. It is simply expressing your need of God in your life. Something happens when we worship God. Worship breaks things off you, chains start to fall, the devil flees, healing takes place, and bondages are broken.

When we go into worship our bodies become a temple prepared for war. Did you ever hear of a war cry? It is when you do not know what to say, but you start to hum a word that is so liberating to your soul. Just the power of that war cry petitions God to get involved in whatever is going on with you. It allows you to get into God's presence and allow him to fight on your behalf.

I love to worship God, chains start to break, and I get free from that which was holding me down. Worship brings you into the presence of God so that he can break bondages off you like depression, worry, anxiety, hurt, pain, rage, anger, and bitterness.

The word 'Worship' is listed 500 times in the bible. What is that saying to you? For the Bible says, 'Therefore God exalted him to the highest place and gave him the name that is above every name, that at the name of Jesus every knee shall bow, in heaven and on earth and under the earth, and every tongue acknowledge that Jesus Christ is Lord, to the glory of God the Father.'

Here are a few worship songs that I truly love:

- Anita Wilson- More Than Anything
- Isabel Davis- The Call
- Isabel Davis- Jesus We Love You
- JJ. Hairston & Youthful Praise- You Deserve It

- Maranda Curtis- Way Maker
- Tasha Cobbs Leonard- Gracefully Broken
- Tasha Cobbs Leonard- You Know My Name ft. Jimi Cravity
- Tasha Cobbs Leonard- Your Spirit ft. Kierra Sheard
- Todd Galberth- Lord You Are Good
- Vashawn Mitchell- My Worship Is for Real

Betrayal and Rejection

Betrayal and rejection come to us all in life at some point. If you have experienced betrayal throughout your life by the ones you love the most, you must ask God what is the purpose behind the betrayal? We know that betrayal and rejection cuts like a knife. Satan tries to mimic Gods' two- edge sword that cuts through bone and marrow. Betrayal is designed by the enemy to bring deception, lying lips, and division in a marriage or any relationship for that matter. A spouse will feel betrayed, rejected, hurt, angry, disrespected, and unappreciated (this is the orphan spirit in other words the spirit of lack or emptiness).

The purpose behind betrayal and rejection is the lack of self-care you give yourself which is needed to become the cure for you. In other words, you fail to be for yourself what you are to others. The same care you gave to others, you need to give it to yourself so that you will not be hurt and bitter after the betrayal and rejection. You should continue in God to love and show others Christ.

The enemy will have you believing that your spouse is the enemy, but you know the devil is a liar, he is truly the father of lies, who is behind the betrayal or rejection. Remember, people are not your enemy. God loves and is concerned about people. Your job is to continue in Christ, the love story by first loving Him, yourself, and then others.

Ephesians 6:12

John 3:16

The betrayal comes to make one feel devalued. It also, alters one's faith, by hindering you from going forth with what God has already given you clear instructions to do. No matter what you do, be obedient, and God will reward you openly.

Psalm 84:11

Deuteronomy 28 1-14

Isaiah 41:13

Did you know that there is a blessing on the other side of betrayal? God is trying to get us to the next level in Him. Sometimes we need to be propelled forward by God or we will be stuck in being complacent. You see, child of God; it is good for us to be made uncomfortable to get to where we need to be.

People who always talk about their circumstances, are the ones who are not filled with God's word to speak it over their lives. My God! You need to ask yourself a few questions. For instance, what word am I speaking over my circumstances? Am I doing the will of God? Prophecy man and woman of God. Speak to those dry bones. We shall live and not die to declare the works of God.

The same love, compassion, and passion that you give to others ask God to return it back to you. When you are constantly praying and being there for others, you too need to be cared for, you need God's healing, this is very important. Also, ask God to deliver you from past hurt, pain, disappointment, bitterness, rage, abuse, and the mistreatment of you immediately. Do not become bitter, but be better, healed, whole, and encourage yourself in the Lord. Build yourself back up, stay full of the word, and attached yourself to the love of God and not His people.

The day you know that you are emotionally healed from the betrayal or rejection is when you can truly pray for that person that caused you the most pain. By praying for that person, you are interceding on their behalf with love and compassion. Child of God, we are to love these difficult people because God loves and creates them for His purpose too. You can even be a friend to that difficult person despite what happened in the past.

Insecurities

Would you say that you are one who is secure in who you are? The truth is everyone on this earth has an insecurity (i.e. Uncertainty or anxiety about oneself; lack of confidence) and are looking for people to validate them.

Sometimes there are many factors that play a role in the insecurities of our lives due to a traumatic experience, event, crisis (loss of a love one, job, injury, divorce, domestic abuse, rape, molestation etc.). Because of these insecurities, one may agree that some people turn to different social media platforms such as Facebook looking for validation.

Insecure people try to adapt to their surroundings so that they will not be the oddball in the crowd, or the one who stands out. They join forces with others to make themselves feel safe and secure. How do you know that you have grown in this area? When you do not get angry when you see this happening amongst family, friends, and you are secure in who you are in Jesus Christ.

When Peter was eating with Paul, he was fine being in the presence of Gentiles, but when other fellow Jews came to the table to eat, Peter acted as if he did not associate with the Gentiles. Paul got mad and confronted Peter about his behavior as a man of God. Back then, the Jews thought they should not eat with Gentiles because if they did, they would have to accept the New Testament, the coming of our Lord and Savior, Jesus Christ. Once again, Peter tries to deny Christ by fitting in with others because he did not want to be judged by the Jews.

Galatians 2:11-13

Galatians 3:28

Validation is just telling you the truth, even if it hurts to save your life. Even UPS must validate your address before shipping the package. Usually, you hear that a man needs validation, but the truth is we all seek it at some point in our lives. My security is anchored in the Lord, Jesus Christ, because He is not a man that he shall lie.

As Christians, why are we looking for something that only Jesus could do for us? Christ validated us at the cross when He said, "It is finished." He was crucified on a cross for you and me. No man can endure what Jesus did on the cross as it was the ultimate sacrifice.

Psalm 139:16

People can relate to Stephen Curry's wife, Ayesha controversies regarding her insecurities, because as a woman she was being one hundred percent real with us. She even said," I need to grow in this area." Jesus Christ accepts us as we are, so He can change us in Him. He knows our beginning to end. He knows how our stories turn out. Why not trust Him with our insecurities and let Him lead and guide us by His Spirit into all truth?

You can get all the plastic surgery money can buy, but you are still left to deal with some insecurities about yourself, therefore, just be who God created you to be. It is hard enough just being you, therefore, why be a replica of someone else? You will make out better just being yourself.

Philippians 4:4-8

Adaptability

Can you adapt and adjust to any environment Jesus Christ place you in? I was having a conversation with my husband who was having a situation at work where the overtime was cancelled out and the men were mad about it for over a week. My husband sees where their concerns lay, and he sees where upper management concerns lay as well.

I realized that God has given my husband the ability to adapt to any environment that God puts him in. When the announcement was pinned on the bulletin board where he works concerning, "No Overtime," the men were mad. Some men even suggested a strike. My husband did not get mad, he simply stated, "Everything happens for a reason and it's not the end of the world."

1 Corinthians 9:22

Adaptability in the dictionary means the quality of being able to adjust to new conditions; having the capacity to be modified for a new use or purpose. In the workplace, your ability to adapt to changing situations and expectations makes you more valuable to a current or prospective employer.

I clearly see that God was saying to my husband, just because he was fine did not mean that co-workers were fine. Everyone does not have the ability to adapt. For some of us, we do not like change. The Holy Spirit will guide and lead you into all truth. Basically, Jesus Christ was saying, "Don't expect others to adapt to something the way you do, because they may not have had the same experiences in life and most importantly, they do not have my Spirit." When we do not realize the power that we have on the inside of us then we start to devalue not only ourselves, but others.

Malachi 3:18

When Jesus is burdening your heart about someone or a situation, our job is to pray for others that they might be saved and delivered. Having a servant's heart is very important. Jesus wants us to pray with clean hands and a pure heart. We need to repent of our arrogance, pride, self-righteousness, and pray for others.

For instance, Esther was okay living in a mansion, getting pampered, eating the best of foods, wearing the best clothes, and jewelry. She was living the good life until her cousin, Mordecai came to tell her that the Jews will be persecuted if she does not do something. She was fine if no harm came to her. Esther's cousin reminded her that the King will soon find out that she was a Jew and she too would be put to death. Esther agreed to go to the King on the Jews behalf, but she first ordered all the Jews to fast, as this was not part of their custom to go before the King unless one was sent for. She could have been put to death, but she had to go anyway. We know how the story ends, with victory.

1 Peter 5:2

How long will we sit pretty on the sideline saying to ourselves, "Oh well, that's them, it's not me?" I have done this whenever my husband was going through trials. I said, "That's his stuff, not mines," but when you are married this is not the case. If one suffers, you both suffer. We are one. The whole time I could have prayed for my husband and found a conflict resolution to save both of us from a heartache, but I did not. Come on people, we have got to get it together as a human race and even more so as people of God.

When Jesus places you in an environment such as sunshine, rain, or snow, He wants you to adapt and adjust so that you will be effective for the Kingdom of God. Jesus knows that He can send you anywhere and that you will be a great effective ministry. Listen, the ministry does not have to only take place in a church, it first starts in our hearts and at home. We are all here on borrowed time. Let us learn, love, pray, and affect this world on a greater level. We must grow, then we can go somewhere.

John 15:16

A Prisoner in Your Own Home

Be careful that you do not become a prisoner in your own home. Stand up for what is right. Remember that a kind word turns away wrath. Speak with a kind and gentle tone to your spouse. I can hear Jesus saying, "My child, for I have equipped you with every tool you will need to live this life." Believe in yourself and know your self-worth. Do not let people walk all over you.

Matthew 5:44

If you are like me and distance yourself from people who get on your nerves, then this message is for you. I get tired sometimes and I shut down in a relationship when I am being overlooked, not heard, or misunderstood. I often stay in my room and do not want to be bothered. You know that you cannot control how other people treat you, but you can control how you respond to the nonsense.

1 Peter 5:8

Take it from me, quite time is not always good, because the enemy wants us isolated to play with your mind. Find a conflict resolution for your problem and do it quickly. I find that talking out your problems and coming up with a solution is the best thing we can do in any relationship.

What if the person you have a problem with does not like controversy? I say, "When the timing and tone of your heart is right, have a conversation." Nothing is worse than being in a relationship and the communication sucks, neither of you wants to get on the same page, or you both just want to be at odds with each other. The enemy will use this as a way in and instigate that situation so that it will be bigger than what it is. I warn you to get out of your comfort zone and speak to your situation and over yourself. Your words have power.

Mark 11:23

I find that when I have prayed about the situation and take time to cool down, I can speak with clarity, peace of mind, and a calmness in my heart. Now, I can speak with love and my spouse can hear me and take everything I say with an open heart.

When they want your Stuff, but they do not Want You

We all have friends and family members who always need something from us, but when the day comes that you need something from them, they do not have it. I cannot tell you how many times I have gotten frustrated and angry over this very thing. It makes me feel used and abused because they were only interested in what I had, not me. I am sure many of you have felt used, abused, and unappreciated many times.

People want what God has for them, but they do not want a personal relationship with Him. They do not want to go through the process of sanctification to receive the blessing they have been praying for either. Be careful that you do not fall into this worldly trap. Jesus says, "I have chosen you and set you apart before the foundations of the world." No one likes trials and tribulations because it tests our faith.

Romans 8:29-30

1 Peter 5:9

I can imagine that Jesus faced this issue on the daily basis. He had many followers, mostly because they needed something from Him. No matter if it was healing, love, or peace, some did not come back to say, "thank you." Remember the story of the ten lepers and only one came back to thank Jesus? How can we be so ungrateful to the one who is and is always there to help us?

Do you know your worth? You are very valuable. When you are worthy to God, people will want your stuff, it is just that simple. We are bought with the blood of Jesus Christ; therefore, we are expensive. Even Jesus wants to know, what are you willing to sacrifice to get what you want? He loves sacrificial prayers, just look at Hanna's story in the bible. How about Joseph? He would not go against the hand of God and sleep with Potiphar's wife, so she lied and had Joseph thrown in jail. Joseph would not sacrifice his integrity or faith in God for a lay in the hay.

Matthew 6:25-27

As good men and women we pay a price for being who we are, that is why the bible says, choose life or death. Jesus says, "Choose this day whom you will serve." When we choose life, we choose to lift and encourage others. We are choosing to love and live a good life that Jesus died to give us. Jesus did not say that we would be exempt from trials and tribulations, but He promises to be with us as we go through the storms of life.

I imagine that Jesus, like most of us feels alone. People love what we can produce, but do not want to spend time to get to know the manufacturer of the goods and services they are receiving. Do not treat God like Santa Clause or an ATM machine, because He is so much more than that. He is our Heavenly Father who loves us unconditionally.

Marriage or Roommate

Which will you choose, marriage or roommate? Do you know the difference between the two? Well, a marriage is everything that God says you can have according to His will. A roommate is someone that you are merely sharing a space with no pressure, or benefits.

I had to ask myself, Daphney which one do you want? Truthfully, for me it would be a marriage. Wives, marriage represents and institution which is family. I do not want to be sleeping in a different room away from my husband and not having any communication with him. The devil is a liar. No thank you God, please restore my marriage.

The enemy will try to use the closes people to you to bring dissension in your marriage. He will use your husband, children, grandchildren, and even the dog. For example, if you have grown children who are still living and now have a child of their own, then it is time for them to get their own place.

Abraham had to kick Hagar and Ishmael out of his home as they were not part of the promise. You know the story of Abraham and Sarah. Hagar was Sarah's handmaid whom she gave Abraham permission to lay with to conceive a child for them. Hagar teased Sarah because she could not have children.

Ishmael is the son of the slave woman (Hagar) and Isaac is the son of the free woman (Sarah). Isaac is the promise child. You were meant to be happy, loved, share quality time together, and raise a family with your spouse. Anything that is going on that is causing problems in your home, you must get rid of it. God does not want us to be unhappy wives.

Another example is if you have younger children, the enemy will try to use them to side with you or your husband by creating dissension. A husband allows his five-year-old daughter to sleep in between him and his wife. Be careful, the wife can become angry because the daughter has her own bed and now, the daughter has learned to do this a few times during the week.

The wife wants to be intimate with her husband or vice versa. We got to recognize what is going on. Dissension and division are happening right in front of their eyes. This is the time to speak with a soft tone, forgive, and say, "Babe" she is old enough to sleep in her own bed, I really need you tonight." Hopefully, husband and wife will be understanding, and no wedge will come between the two.

In marriage, I believe that both spouses must be loving, compassionate, and speak kind words to each other. As women, we tend to get emotionally upset and speak from our damage places because of something that happened in our past. Men tend to shut down communication when a woman is emotionally distraught. He cannot handle it, he does not want to hear it, or he just does not know how to fix it.

We all need to learn to forgive and speak from a higher level called plentiful in us instead of the lower level that I like to call the reservoir, or emptiness.

Matthew 18:21-22

Proverbs 15:1

1 Peter 4:8

Hebrews 3:13

Living versus Existing

I heard this phrase one day, "Are you living or just existing?" It is so important to do a self-evaluation every now and then. Jesus talked in parables. I love the story of the farmer who was planting seeds one day. Some seed fell and were crushed, other seeds were eaten by the birds, some fell on stony ground, and so forth.

Jesus is talking about the condition of our hearts. We let so much junk into our hearts that there is no room for God's word to live or grow inside of us. We are suffocating the Holy Spirit and thus not really living a life of purpose. The human heart is like a rich soil. Things like our thoughts, ideas, attitudes, past hurts, and pains live there daily. I want you to picture the most beautiful, colorful garden you can ever imagine. Now, imagine that garden slowly dying and all the colors just fading away. Sadly, to say that picture after while looks like everything in the garden died.

Great news for you and me, if we are willing to give our hearts over to God and ask Him to plant and water the seed, He will get the increase bringing us back to life. You will get a clean heart and God will get the Glory. When we yield our hearts to God, we are living life or purpose, otherwise, we just exist. I do not know about you, but I want more out of life than just existing. I want to dance, sing, shout, and celebrate to the break of dawn.

We all need to do a self-examination daily. When was the last time you laughed, danced, dated yourself, or even loved yourself? I was going to family gatherings and not really enjoying myself. One day I said to myself, "no more," and I heard a song my father use to play by Frankie Beverly and Maze "Before I let Go" at a block party. I got up started grooving. Do you know that I danced three songs in a row and laughed so hard that I could not breathe? Listen, I did not care who saw me, I was loving on me. I had so much fun that night and I decided that I want to live, not just merely exist in this world.

Live baby live! Get up, go for a walk, smell the flowers, watch the butterflies, and lightening bugs light-up. God wants us to be happy and live a long and prosperous life. It is so worth your while to step out on faith and live. Do not be cooped up in the house continuing to be bored weekend after weekend. Live because we only get one life, so enjoy it to the fullest.

Luke 8:4-15

John 10:10

Psalms 51:10

Co-dependency

We are all co-dependents, whether we believe it or not. Let us face it, some people hate it, but it is the way God created some things to be, especially in marriage.

In work relationships, you cannot do your work if you need a component of that work from a person who may be away on vacation. You cannot do your job since you need a very important document from that person. The missing document would have completed your task at hand. Now, you have a problem!

You cannot jump over it, go under it, or around it. You must wait it out because you need your co-worker. Check-in with your feelings and motives because you cannot get mad, the situation is what it is. The best practice you can do is move on to another small task until that person returns with the document you need to complete the priority task at hand.

Isaiah 41:10

Often, in marriages, you cannot get ahead without your spouse. How can they walk together except they agree? Once you say, "I Do," God makes you both co-dependent on one another. Meaning you cannot get ahead unless you both get ahead.

You must work together for a common goal or it will not work. You cannot make any major decisions without your spouse. In this type of relationship, God requires the husband and wife to make decisions together concerning the family and finances. Husbands and wives need to complement and strengthen each other.

Ephesians 5:21-31

Philippians 2:1-5

We must remember that although we must be co-dependent on one another, your spouse cannot take the place of God in your life. Only God can fulfill every need we have and come through in our lives when no one else can.

On the other hand, being too co-dependent on our spouse can be negative. This means that co-dependency is deeply rooted in a person in a negative way (i.e. Due to the insecurities in their life).

In this type of relationship, a partner may not like the way things are, but refuses to leave the relationship due to fear of being alone. Here are five ways to uproot that negative spirit:

1. Create healthy boundaries.
2. Know that it is not possible to control another person. You can only be responsible for what you do. Use boundaries to detach with love. Trying to control another person through fixing them, manipulating them, or enabling them is essentially living in dysfunction.
3. Create your happiness and know that another person is not responsible for your happiness. Look to Jesus to supply your every need.
4. Work on your self-esteem. Jesus never had low self-esteem because He knows who He is and to whom He belongs.
5. Do not let your emotions control you. Know that you cannot go through life counting on a feeling to move you this way or that way.
6. Make sure that you always have the right motives and you will always have a positive outcome no matter the situation.
7. Be optimistic, not pessimistic.

To become less co-dependent is knowing who you are in God, knowing your worth, and wanting happiness for yourself and others around you. Now, do not get me wrong, we must have balance in all we do. We cannot get this type of co-dependency confused with being independent as if we are not married.

Please know that we are not responsible for someone else's happiness, nor are we to just run off making our own decisions without talking to our spouse first. Our happiness is something we must work out apart from our spouse. They cannot be Jesus for you nor can you be Jesus for them, therefore, they must seek their own happiness which is wrapped up in Jesus Christ alone.

Care about yourself enough to do the things that make you happy. This does not make you selfish or single minded. It shows that you understand that if you are happy you can brighten up the atmosphere around you which helps others to find their own joy.

Here are seven ways to self-care for yourself:

1. Love yourself and get to know who you are, who Jesus is, and know that you belong to Him. Even in marriage, you need to still have that independent part of you that you loved outside of the relationship. We all need some alone time.
2. Believe in God, yourself, and believe the best in others.
3. Be assertive, let your "Yes" be yes and your "No" be no.
4. Start making your own decisions by taking everything to Jesus in prayer and trusting Him to guide you in the right direction.
5. Know that God will supply all your needs, not your spouse.
6. Learn to do things that make you feel better about you (i.e. Massage, hot bubble bath, glass of wine, go out to eat by yourself).
7. Know that everything does not require a response. Be quiet and listen more.

Now, I know I have said a lot, but just know the most important part is to follow and rely on Jesus. There is a thin line between good and bad when it comes to co-dependency in a marriage. Make sure you allow God to guide you and keep you on the healthy co-dependency track. Keep balance in the forefront of your mind.

God promises to love us forever. By putting your trust in man, you will always fall short. Your full trust should be in God and He will lead you. Please do not put your spouse on a pedestal because he or she is not God.

Jeremiah 31:3

Believe

Do you believe God? If God said it, then it is your job to believe it. He is all mighty God who watches over His word to perform it. God is not a man that He should lie. Remember, the Word is powerful in your life. If it were not so, He would not have told you.

Isaiah 55:11

Those who believe that Jesus died on the cross and He shed His blood made us right with God shall have everlasting life. He died for you and me. God loves us unconditionally. He will never leave us or forsake us.

Just trust God even when you do not trust yourself or anyone else for that matter. He is so loving and caring. God has plans to prosper you not to harm you and to bring you to an expected end (His outcomes are better than yours).

Romans 8:31-34

Do you know how long, how deep, how wide God's love is for us? There is nothing that can separate us from the love of God. Do you believe? We are victorious! We are a chosen people and a royal priesthood.

Ephesians 3:18-19

If God is for us, who can be against us. God loves us so much. If there were a hundred sheep on the hill and one runs away, He will leave the ninety-nine to go after that one. He will then rejoice when He finds it! God loves us enough that He will not give up on us.

Matthew 18:12-13

In the end, let us take God at His word and be obedient so that we can be rewarded. God loves to bless His children. Praise God from whom all our blessings flow. You know His word is tested, tried, and proven true. His word does not come back void. Believe!

Victim Mindset versus Kingdom Mindset

There are so many people walking around today with burdens that are so heavy that you will never know. Emotional healing is detrimental to our lives. When we are walking around with issues from the past that way us down, we cannot get to the next stage of life.

Walking around with all that weight makes us easy targets for the enemy who takes pride in using our past against us. The enemy is banking on you to never forgive that person or situation that hurt you, which will cause you to deny God and whatever blessings He has for you.

1 Peter 5:8

Do you know what we conceal, Jesus will not heal? As people of God, we find that as we evolve in life the bitterness, anger, and fears start to spill over in our lives and starts to reveal itself through that drug, alcohol, and food addiction.

Emotional healing is very important and needed at various stages of our lives depending on what season we are in. There are people who have Daddy and Mommy issues where they were never present in the home for whatever reason. Jesus says, "Cast your cares (burdens) on me for I care for you."

1 Peter 5:7

Matthew 11:28-30

Having a victim mindset is a person who never sees the part they played in a situation. They think everyone is out to get them because of a trauma they faced in the past. They will go to great lengths to defend themselves in ways you could never imagine. This person is always concerned about themselves, not getting hurt again that they do not care if they hurt the next in the process. A person who always plays the victim does not see or know a way out of their situation, so they will make up things that are not true. How many people know that Jesus always gives us a safe way out?

Romans 8:37-38

A person that has a kingdom mindset is one who abounds in love, who is confident, who knows that only Jesus validates them. Jesus said abide in me and I will abide in you. In other words, we are the branches that need to stay connected to the vine who is Jesus, the true way and light. Apart from Jesus, we cannot do anything.

Jesus is the reason for any season. He is our happiness, joy, strength, peace, love, and so much more. We need Jesus like we need the air we breathe. Jesus is healing and wholeness to our hellish souls.

Nehemiah 8:10

1 Corinthians 15:57

Mistreated

If Jesus was mistreated all the way to the cross, what makes you think that you are exempt? Just because we are Christians, does not mean that we go unscathed in this life. We too must face many trials and tribulations, just like Jesus Christ.

Betrayal and rejection take place in your life for many reasons. The Lord Jesus Christ was betrayed and rejected, therefore, if we are His children, then we too must share in His sufferings. Jesus was mistreated in many ways. He was bruised for our iniquities. The mistreatment of our Lord and Savior, Jesus Christ, was unbearable! Yet, He still died for you and me.

These things happened so that the prophecies in scripture would be fulfilled. I often think about people who mistreated or mistreat me and no matter what I cannot hate them. Jesus teaches us to pray for those who persecute and despitefully use us.

There is beauty in betrayal and rejection. It happens so that...

1. You will know God
2. You will trust God
3. Take everything to God in prayer
4. Trust God to handle others- He says, "Vengeance is mine"
5. You will witness the betrayer hang him or herself every time

Isaiah 53:5

Philippians 4:6-7

Romans 12:14-21

God is the beauty in our betrayal and rejection!

Prophesy

Speak Women and Men of God! Speak in your home, over your life, spouse, children, family, workplace, and more. To prophesy is to speak the mind and heart of God. One part of the prophesy is to speak the future into existence just as God did at the beginning of time when He created the Heavens and the earth. Then prophesy the life you want, and God will fulfill it according to His perfect will for your life.

1 Corinthians 13:9

God said to me, "We got to open our mouths and speak those things as if they were." Back in the Old Testament, there were prophets who would deliver God's messages. In the New Testament, God sent His only son, Jesus, to do so much more. What I am trying to say is, the same power that worked in Jesus is working in you and me. When Jesus went to sit at the right-hand of the Father, he left you and I the Holy Spirit to help guide and lead us to our destiny.

As a wife, mother, and grandmother, I have learned to speak over those things which concerns me, and I will tell you that our words have power. I do not know about you, but as for me and my house, we will serve the Lord. Life and death are in the power of our tongues and those that love the fruit will eat it thereof. We have a choice to speak life or death.

Psalm 34:1

We really need to "watch our mouths," because what we speak out into the atmosphere carries significant weight and could come back to bite us in the butt. I was listening to a well-known preacher, Dr. Cindy Trim spoke on a YouTube video and she said, "Start saying 'I' phrases," like:

- I am wonderfully and beautifully made
- I am enveloped with the Holy Spirit
- I am a child of righteousness
- I share in the inheritance of Jesus
- I have favor with God and Men
- I am anointed
- I am blessed and highly favored
- I am loved unconditionally

Dr. Cindy Trim said, "Don't speak any "You" phrases to yourself," meaning:

- You do not know
- You cannot
- You need help
- You are not this or that

If you speak "You," phrases out into the atmosphere, you are binding yourself and you will not soar in life. We have got to get into the practice of speaking the right things. We must allow God's word to wash our limited mindsets away and that comes with renewing our minds daily. Do you know that it is not about what people think of us, but what we think of ourselves that keeps us bond?

Psalm 139:14

Luke1:28

2 Corinthians 12:10

Life is not a Sprint or a Marathon

Sitting next to a co-worker on the shuttle bus to work, she decided to tell me that she is dumping her boyfriend of only seven months. I asked her why and she said, she does not feel the excitement or romance she experienced in the beginning of the relationship. She said, she was not into him even though he has a nice body. She just does not feel the spark with him anymore. She mentioned that she had been in several relationships and she knows what she wants.

When I was in my twenties, I too dumped a guy after being with him for only seven months. The love, excitement and romance were not there. He wasn't the one that I could not bear to live without. One day, I found myself in the kitchen crying my eyes out. I did not know what was wrong with me. Looking back on it, I was unhappy with my life and the choices I had made.

We both had a daughter from previous relationships. My daughter was four years old and his daughter was five years old. When his daughter came over for a playdate, our daughters did not get along well. To make a long story short, I broke up with him.

Now, I can totally relate to my co-worker. As a wise woman today, I would recommend not getting into a relationship until you have learned who you are. It is important to know your likes, dislikes, and what you are passionate about.

People, please know that you cannot change an individual. You can only make suggestions on how this or that might work for the person verses trying to change or control them. Only God can change hearts and minds, not you.

In life, we have relationships that are assets, and some are liabilities. Know that each person that comes into your life has a purpose and is there for a season or a lifetime.

Do not waste valuable time sprinting through life because it is not a marathon. Be wise about who you are and what you want. Beware of the company you keep, work on your spiritual life, and most importantly, be selfless and treat people how you would want to be treated.

Ecclesiastes 9:11

Title versus Entitled

Are you entitled just because of your title as husband, wife, son, daughter, pastor, deacon, deaconess, etc.? We are inheritance to the throne because of our Lord and Savior, Jesus Christ, therefore, we are entitled to whatever our Heavenly Father has for us. Remember, God doesn't owe us anything, but because He loves us He gives freely so humble yourself.

Romans 8:17

Do you get caught up in titles? Have you heard the saying, "A man makes the clothes he wears not the clothes make a man?" In other words, just because you have a huge title does not mean you are entitled to anything. People are not entitled just because of their title. At the end of the day, people with huge titles are human and are going to make mistakes just like people with small or no titles at all.

Like anything in life, you must work hard at it if you want it to last or stand the test of time. For example, a good relationship, promotion, dinner at a nice restaurant, college degree, or etc.

- Do not expect peaches when you planted grapes or tomatoes when you planted potatoes. People always want to know, "What did I do?" Un-expectantly, people are surprised when they get a low-grade response. If you don't praise them the way they want, you too, then they are mad. These people think they are entitled because of a title or who they are.

- Do not expect someone to behave in a certain manner just because they carry an important title like for instance, "Deacon, Minister, Pastor, Doctor, Lawyer, President, etc." You can have a high respectable title and be a complete jerk.

- Do not expect a loving relationship when you treat your spouse less than. Basically, you get out of a relationship what you put into it. If you want your relationship to grow, then you will simply work with your spouse in a loving and understanding way to build a lasting relationship and home. The benefits are a win, win for you both. No one likes to lose.

Listen, we are all human and fall short of the glory of God every day. Hold Jesus Christ in high regard not people.

Romans 3:23

Escalates versus De-Escalates

Why do we get so angry at each other? Anger can be deeply rooted in our hearts due to past hurts and pains. Do not hold anger inside due to unresolved issues that you could have dealt with when it happened. The best thing to do is to remain calm and use your discretion. To make sound decisions you must have a sound mind.

Ecclesiastes 10:1

Do not let your anger escalate, but de-escalate so that you will be able to think clearly. There is something called righteous anger. You can have the right to be mad, but do not sin in your anger. Keeping your cool will help you to make clear and wise decisions. This requires one to always be focused on the things of God.

Philippians 4:7

When your head is cloudy, you are more prone to make bad decisions like saying something extreme that you cannot take back. You are prone to listen to a stranger over your spouse (who by the way is not your enemy), this should not be the case.

Ecclesiastes 9:17-18

Ephesians 6:12

We must be wise and know that God will not put more on us than we can handle because His burdens are light. Put your trust in the one who has given His life so that you can live. Remember, Jesus died on the cross for you and me. Go boldly to the throne of grace and tell God, what is on your heart. He knows what you need before you even ask it, but He always loves to hear your voice. Plus, He wants to give you clear instructions that will help you greatly.

Ecclesiastes 10:2

Cast your cares on God as He truly loves and wants the best for you. God will have your best interest at heart. Trust God with all your heart, soul, and mind. Stop focusing on what you do not have and praise Him for what you do have. Be thankful and grateful towards God throughout your day for all that He has already done. He owes us nothing.

Matthew 11:28-30

Philippians 4:11

Be Still

What is impossible with man is possible with God. Putting your trust in man will prove to be a snare or trap. How can you lay down next to your spouse knowing that he or she is the betrayer? Jesus knew Judas was going to betray him. Judas went and talked to the chief priests and others about Jesus, whom he loved and vice versa. Judas worked as the treasurer among the disciples. Satan used the money to bate Judas. We cannot serve money and God, so we must love one and hate the other.

Remember the woman with the alabaster box? The box contained expensive perfume worth a year's wages. She sacrificed it just to pour it on Jesus' head and to wash His feet with her tears and hair. "She was actually preparing my body for burial, says Jesus," to Judas.

God resurrected Jesus in three days. Jesus said go get my disciples and Peter. We all know that Peter denied Him three times. We can betray, deny, walk away from Jesus, but He still loves us. Jesus sees the best in each of us always.

When we are weak, He is strong. When we are being tested, we are at our weakest. Jesus tests our faith and Satan temps us to sin. Be still and know that He is God. Trust Him! Wives do not vent to your girlfriends on the phone. Husbands do not vent on social media, and do not get angry knowing you cannot achieve anything in your human strength. Know that this test is spiritual not carnal or natural. Get out of your feelings, get out of your head, and get into God's presence, because that's where things change.

Spiritual warfare is real people and we keep trying to fight with our human strength that causes us to lose and go back to square one. We must trust Jesus no matter how bad, dead, or stinky our situation gets, Lazarus. Only Jesus could achieve the miracle that you need! Only Jesus can bring you and/or your spouse out of the dead places, not you. Your job is to pray and trust your Heavenly Father to bring you through.

Remember, He is strong when you are weak. Jesus says, "Untie her and lose her now." No matter how many days you have been dead, buried, and started to decay you have resurrection power on the inside of you. His name is Jesus Christ!

Psalms 46:10

Proverbs 29:25

James 1:19

Let us Get Back to the Basics

The spread of the Coronavirus happened during the Spring of 2020; I believe because God wants this world to get back to the basics. The basics are simply Him. This world is out of order. God is missing from our schools, our homes, and our lives, period. No one has time for God anymore, but they want Him to be there at there every beacon call. Listen, God is not Santa Clause where we give Him a list of what we want, and He goes and bring it back on a sleigh.

One of God's love languages is "Quality Time." When was the last time you stole away in a secret place to spend time with God? When was the last time you read and studied His Word? Don't you know that He is a jealous God and He do not want you to put anything or anyone before Him? Not you, your spouse, children, church, hobbies, food, sex, or anything that will take from His relationship with you. We are robbing God and not just in our tithe and offering, but our time.

Malachi 3:10

God sent His Spirit to reside in our hearts. We go to church, pray over our food, read a couple of scriptures, and we think we in right standing with God. Do not be fooled like the five virgins who ran out of oil.

Matthew 25:5-13

We go to church to shout, praise, dance, and to hear a good sermon, even Satan attends church and he knows the word better than us. "You are a stench in my nostrils," says God. Now, church and bible study are available online. You can watch from home lying in your bed. Listen, we are missing the whole experience of God all together. You better get to know Him because God is for real and He is coming back again.

Who knew that He would use the Coronavirus (COVID-19) to get the world's attention? He got mine, how about yours? Don't you love God? What is wrong with you? Come on all these gifts and talents the Holy Spirit has given to us, where is our wisdom? When are we going to repent, so Jesus can hear from heaven and heal our land? We need The Most-High God because there is no other like Him!

Matthew 19:26

Depression

Depression is feelings of severe despondency and dejection; self-doubt creeps in and that swiftly turns to depression. A mood disorder that causes a persistent feeling of sadness and loss of interest. This is also called major depressive disorder or clinical depression. It affects how you feel, think, and behave and can lead to a variety of emotional (distress) and physical problems.

For me, depression came as self-doubt. It seems impossible to complete an assignment when you have so much opposition against you. I heard God say, "You are not doing this correctly, seek my face, chase after me, steal away with me, stay prayerful, and stay hopeful." I have done all of that and I still do not have. God says, "Could you have prayed amidst?" Did you pray with pure motives?

James 4:3

Ephesians 1:18

What happens if you get weary? For me, I get into bed and pull the covers over my face, unable to sleep, just lying there resting. No one comes to my rescue, baby I am on my own. I try reasoning in my head with myself and here comes self-doubt creeping in, why?

Because there were already fortified strongholds in my mind that was never torn down, therefore, the enemy creeps in suddenly. He loves to come back and tap into those hurting places. The enemy loves to resurrect those old dead places in you to get you to fall. Satan loves to get Christians kicked out of the Kingdom of God.

If we do not deal with the strongholds in our lives, we will be defeated every time. I have prayed and asked God to remove the scandals in my soul which are the planted seeds of the enemy in my mind.

How do I know God was not using this time in my life to deal with one or two of my strongholds? All I knew, was I felt helpless and no one came to my aid. This was the time in my life in which I learned that people do not always have what I need, only God. I cannot get juice from a turnip. I must go to the source, my God.

Philippians 4:19

2 Corinthians 12:9-11

Because God got up with all power in His hands, we can get up. We have resurrection power that lives on the inside of us. He is not like no other! God is awesome, mighty in power, my strong tower, my peace, the joy of the Lord is my strength, my provider, my healer, and so much more. I heard God say, "I'm in control, not you my daughter. Remember my covenant and do not betray me, yourself, or others. Hate the enemy, not man."

Child of God, we must speak over ourselves and our circumstances. Failure to do so, allows the enemy to creep in to kill, steal, and destroy. Take back your power as the enemy is a defeated foe, and remember you are a child of The Most High God.

John 10:10

Matthew 28:18

Choosing My Own Way

How many of you out there are just stubborn like me? When God tells us to go one way and we choose our own way. You know there is always going to be interruptions in our lives.

I believed in my mind that my husband has done sneaky things behind my back for so long that it became my truth. God specifically told me to watch my mouth! The bible says, "So a man thinks, so he is." My thoughts were becoming my truths. Then asked me, what did I do? I opened my mouth and said things to my husband, I should not have.

Romans 12:3

Proverbs 23:7

Proverbs 1:31

My bad behavior and misconduct caused me to go into depression mode. I for one, do not like looking stupid and just plain down right out of control. You know, once you say something you cannot take it back. The words that we speak are powerful and they move in motion to do just what we say. I stayed in my bedroom all day, not wanting to eat.

For me this is not cool, I can count on one hand how many times I have slipped into a depression. I do not like to be in that space at all. Now, I am back at square one trying to work out my own salvation. You know you cannot get your life back on track until you repent and give that situation over to God.

Proverbs 18:21

Psalms 33:9

Romans 14:7

If we lean not on our own understanding and recognize what God is saying and doing, we would be better off. The problem is that we want to be in control of every area of our lives, but He created us, so He has rights over us. We did not create Him.

A big part of my test was relinquishing that control I thought I had over my mind, heart, my soul, and my marriage over to God. When He is running things, our lives are a whole lot smoother. If we just listen to what our Heavenly Father says, we would be so much further along in life than where we are now. The best thing about God is, He is so loving and patient with us, and will wait until we wear ourselves out trying to do only what He can do.

Today, it took me getting on a prayer line to ask my Sisters in Christ to pray on my behalf for my marriage, because I could not do it. One of my sisters said, "God, I pray that she cries out to you Lord and give her situation over to you." Finally, I felt the tugging of the Lord pulling on my heart strings and I began to cry out to the Lord. I felt like I could not eat, sleep, or anything until I had turned everything over to the Lord.

Philippians 4:13

Jeremiah 32:27

Thessalonians 5:24

Psalms 138:8

God is waiting on us to come to Him. He loves us with an everlasting love that will never die. Just turn it all over to Jesus. He is the way, the truth, and the life. We must stay connected to our source which is God from whom all blessings flow. Jesus will never steer us wrong. Everything the Father does is deeply rooted in love. Be blessed and most importantly Godly wives be encouraged.

www.ingramcontent.com/pod-product-compliance
Lightning Source LLC
Chambersburg PA
CBHW071005080526
44587CB00015B/2358